50 Dreamy Dessert Recipes for Home

By: Kelly Johnson

Table of Contents

- Classic Vanilla Ice Cream
- Chocolate Fudge Brownie Sundae
- Strawberry Cheesecake Sorbet
- Mango Coconut Gelato
- Mint Chocolate Chip Ice Cream
- Raspberry Lemonade Granita
- Salted Caramel Swirl Frozen Yogurt
- Blueberry Basil Sorbet
- Peanut Butter Cup Ice Cream
- Pina Colada Sorbet
- Matcha Green Tea Ice Cream
- Cookies and Cream Gelato
- Peach Melba Granita
- Mocha Almond Fudge Ice Cream
- Pineapple Coconut Frozen Smoothie
- Raspberry White Chocolate Gelato
- Lemon Basil Sorbet
- Hazelnut Coffee Ice Cream
- Blackberry Mint Frozen Yogurt
- Cinnamon Roll Ice Cream
- Watermelon Mint Granita
- Pumpkin Spice Frozen Custard
- Chocolate Raspberry Sorbet
- Almond Joy Gelato
- Key Lime Pie Frozen Yogurt
- Espresso Affogato
- Cherry Vanilla Ice Cream
- Tropical Fruit Sorbet
- Nutella Swirl Gelato
- Spiced Apple Frozen Smoothie
- Hibiscus Raspberry Sorbet
- Caramel Macchiato Ice Cream
- Lemon Blueberry Cheesecake Gelato
- White Chocolate Ginger Frozen Yogurt
- Classic Strawberry Ice Cream
- Mango Passionfruit Sorbet

- Tiramisu Gelato
- Fig and Honey Ice Cream
- Matcha Red Bean Sorbet
- S'mores Frozen Custard
- Pineapple Mint Gelato
- Chai Tea Ice Cream
- Pear Vanilla Sorbet
- Dark Chocolate Chili Ice Cream
- Coconut Lychee Gelato
- Blackberry Lemonade Granita
- Banana Cream Pie Gelato
- Classic Pistachio Gelato
- Maple Pecan Ice Cream
- Matcha Lemon Sorbet

Classic Vanilla Ice Cream

Ingredients:

- 2 cups whole milk
- 1 cup heavy cream
- 3/4 cup granulated sugar
- 1 tablespoon vanilla extract
- 4 large egg yolks
- A pinch of salt

Instructions:

1. **Heat Milk and Cream:**
    1. In a medium saucepan, combine the whole milk and heavy cream. Heat over medium heat until it begins to steam but does not boil.
2. **Whisk Egg Yolks and Sugar:**
    1. In a separate bowl, whisk together the granulated sugar and egg yolks until smooth and pale.
3. **Temper Egg Yolks:**
    1. Gradually whisk a small amount of the warm milk mixture into the egg yolks to temper them.
    2. Return the egg yolk mixture to the saucepan with the remaining milk mixture.
4. **Cook Custard Base:**
    1. Cook the mixture over medium heat, stirring constantly, until it thickens slightly and coats the back of a spoon (about 5-7 minutes). Do not let it boil.
5. **Add Vanilla and Cool:**
    1. Remove the saucepan from heat and stir in the vanilla extract and a pinch of salt.
    2. Pour the custard base through a fine-mesh sieve into a clean bowl to remove any lumps.
    3. Allow the mixture to cool to room temperature.
6. **Chill:**
    1. Cover and refrigerate the custard base for at least 2 hours, or until thoroughly chilled.
7. **Churn:**
    1. Pour the chilled mixture into an ice cream maker and churn according to the manufacturer's instructions. This usually takes about 20-25 minutes, or until the ice cream reaches a soft-serve consistency.
8. **Freeze:**
    1. Transfer the churned ice cream to an airtight container.
    2. Freeze for at least 2 hours, or until firm.
9. **Serve:**
    1. Scoop and enjoy your classic vanilla ice cream!

Indulge in the timeless, creamy taste of classic vanilla ice cream—simple, delicious, and always a favorite!

Chocolate Fudge Brownie Sundae

Ingredients:

For the Brownies:

- 1/2 cup unsalted butter
- 1 cup granulated sugar
- 2 large eggs
- 1/2 cup unsweetened cocoa powder
- 1/2 cup all-purpose flour
- 1/4 teaspoon salt
- 1/4 teaspoon baking powder
- 1/2 cup semi-sweet chocolate chips

For the Fudge Sauce:

- 1/2 cup heavy cream
- 1/2 cup semi-sweet chocolate chips
- 1 tablespoon light corn syrup
- 1/2 teaspoon vanilla extract

For the Sundae:

- 2 cups vanilla ice cream
- 1/2 cup chocolate fudge sauce (from above)
- Whipped cream (optional)
- Maraschino cherries (optional)
- Additional brownie pieces for garnish (optional)

Instructions:

1. **Prepare the Brownies:**
    1. Preheat your oven to 350°F (175°C). Grease and flour an 8x8-inch baking pan.
    2. In a microwave-safe bowl, melt the unsalted butter in the microwave.
    3. Stir in the granulated sugar until well combined.
    4. Add the eggs one at a time, beating well after each addition.
    5. Mix in the unsweetened cocoa powder, flour, salt, and baking powder until just combined.
    6. Fold in the semi-sweet chocolate chips.
    7. Pour the batter into the prepared baking pan and spread evenly.
    8. Bake for 20-25 minutes, or until a toothpick inserted into the center comes out with a few moist crumbs. Allow to cool completely before cutting into squares.
2. **Prepare the Fudge Sauce:**
    1. In a small saucepan, heat the heavy cream over medium heat until it begins to simmer.

2. Remove from heat and add the semi-sweet chocolate chips and light corn syrup.
   3. Stir until the chocolate is fully melted and the sauce is smooth.
   4. Stir in the vanilla extract. Allow to cool slightly before using.
3. **Assemble the Sundae:**
   1. Place a scoop of vanilla ice cream into each serving bowl or dish.
   2. Cut the brownies into bite-sized pieces and place them on top of the ice cream.
   3. Drizzle with the warm chocolate fudge sauce.
   4. Add whipped cream and maraschino cherries if desired.
   5. Garnish with additional brownie pieces if you like.
4. **Serve:**
   1. Enjoy your indulgent Chocolate Fudge Brownie Sundae immediately!

Savor the rich combination of chocolate fudge, gooey brownie pieces, and creamy vanilla ice cream in this decadent sundae!

Strawberry Cheesecake Sorbet

Ingredients:

For the Strawberry Puree:

- 2 cups fresh or frozen strawberries, hulled
- 1/2 cup granulated sugar (adjust based on sweetness of strawberries)
- 1 tablespoon freshly squeezed lemon juice

For the Cheesecake Mixture:

- 1/2 cup cream cheese, softened
- 1/2 cup plain Greek yogurt or sour cream
- 1/2 cup granulated sugar
- 1 teaspoon vanilla extract
- 1/2 cup water

Instructions:

1. **Prepare Strawberry Puree:**
    1. In a blender or food processor, blend the strawberries until smooth.
    2. Add the granulated sugar and lemon juice, blending until well combined. Taste and adjust sweetness if needed.
    3. Strain the strawberry puree through a fine-mesh sieve into a bowl to remove seeds and any pulp. Set aside.
2. **Prepare Cheesecake Mixture:**
    1. In a medium bowl, beat the softened cream cheese until smooth and creamy.
    2. Add the plain Greek yogurt (or sour cream), granulated sugar, and vanilla extract. Beat until well combined and smooth.
    3. Gradually mix in the water until the mixture is smooth and easily pourable.
3. **Combine Mixtures:**
    1. Gently fold the strawberry puree into the cheesecake mixture until fully combined. Be careful not to overmix to maintain a swirl effect if desired.
4. **Chill Mixture:**
    1. Cover the mixture and refrigerate for at least 1-2 hours, or until thoroughly chilled.
5. **Freeze Sorbet:**
    1. Pour the chilled mixture into an ice cream maker and churn according to the manufacturer's instructions. This usually takes about 20-25 minutes, or until the sorbet reaches a soft-serve consistency.
6. **Freeze:**
    1. Transfer the churned sorbet to an airtight container. Freeze for at least 2 hours, or until firm.
7. **Serve:**

1. Scoop and enjoy your refreshing Strawberry Cheesecake Sorbet! Garnish with fresh strawberries or a mint sprig if desired.

Enjoy the delightful combination of creamy cheesecake and fruity strawberry sorbet in every delicious bite!

Mango Coconut Gelato

Mango Coconut Gelato

Ingredients:

For the Mango Base:

- 2 cups fresh or frozen mango chunks (thawed if frozen)
- 1/2 cup granulated sugar
- 1 tablespoon freshly squeezed lime juice
- 1/2 teaspoon vanilla extract

For the Coconut Mixture:

- 1 cup full-fat coconut milk
- 1 cup heavy cream
- 1/2 cup granulated sugar
- 1/4 cup shredded coconut (optional, for extra texture)
- 1/4 teaspoon salt

Instructions:

1. **Prepare Mango Base:**
    1. In a blender or food processor, combine the mango chunks, granulated sugar, lime juice, and vanilla extract. Blend until smooth.
    2. Taste and adjust sweetness or lime juice as needed. Set aside.
2. **Prepare Coconut Mixture:**
    1. In a medium bowl, whisk together the full-fat coconut milk, heavy cream, and granulated sugar until the sugar is fully dissolved.
    2. Stir in the shredded coconut and salt until well combined.
3. **Combine Mixtures:**
    1. Gently fold the mango puree into the coconut mixture until fully combined. Be careful not to overmix.
4. **Chill Mixture:**
    1. Cover the mixture and refrigerate for at least 1-2 hours, or until thoroughly chilled.
5. **Churn Gelato:**
    1. Pour the chilled mixture into an ice cream maker and churn according to the manufacturer's instructions. This usually takes about 20-25 minutes, or until the gelato reaches a creamy, soft-serve consistency.
6. **Freeze:**
    1. Transfer the churned gelato to an airtight container. Freeze for at least 2 hours, or until firm.
7. **Serve:**
    1. Scoop and enjoy your Mango Coconut Gelato! Garnish with extra shredded coconut or fresh mango slices if desired.

Experience the tropical blend of creamy coconut and sweet mango in this delightful and refreshing gelato!

Mint Chocolate Chip Ice Cream

Ingredients:

For the Mint Base:

- 2 cups whole milk
- 1 cup heavy cream
- 3/4 cup granulated sugar
- 1 teaspoon vanilla extract
- 1 teaspoon peppermint extract (adjust to taste)
- A few drops of green food coloring (optional, for color)

For the Chocolate Chips:

- 1/2 cup semi-sweet chocolate chips or chopped chocolate

Instructions:

1. **Prepare the Mint Base:**
    1. In a medium saucepan, combine the whole milk and heavy cream. Heat over medium heat until it begins to steam but does not boil.
    2. In a separate bowl, whisk together the granulated sugar until fully dissolved.
    3. Remove the saucepan from heat and stir in the sugar until fully dissolved.
    4. Stir in the vanilla extract, peppermint extract, and green food coloring (if using).
2. **Chill Mixture:**
    1. Allow the mixture to cool to room temperature.
    2. Cover and refrigerate for at least 2 hours, or until thoroughly chilled.
3. **Churn Ice Cream:**
    1. Pour the chilled mixture into an ice cream maker and churn according to the manufacturer's instructions. This usually takes about 20-25 minutes, or until it reaches a soft-serve consistency.
    2. During the last few minutes of churning, add the chocolate chips or chopped chocolate to the ice cream maker to mix in evenly.
4. **Freeze:**
    1. Transfer the churned ice cream to an airtight container.
    2. Freeze for at least 2 hours, or until firm.
5. **Serve:**
    1. Scoop and enjoy your Mint Chocolate Chip Ice Cream! For a touch of extra mintiness, you can garnish with fresh mint leaves.

Indulge in the refreshing flavor of mint combined with rich chocolate chips in this classic, creamy ice cream!

Raspberry Lemonade Granita

Ingredients:

- 2 cups fresh raspberries (or thawed frozen raspberries)
- 1 cup freshly squeezed lemon juice (about 4-5 lemons)
- 3/4 cup granulated sugar
- 1 cup water
- 1 teaspoon lemon zest (optional, for extra flavor)
- A pinch of salt

Instructions:

1. **Prepare Raspberry Puree:**
    1. In a blender or food processor, blend the raspberries until smooth.
    2. Strain the raspberry puree through a fine-mesh sieve into a bowl to remove seeds and pulp.
2. **Prepare Lemonade Mixture:**
    1. In a medium bowl, combine the freshly squeezed lemon juice, granulated sugar, and water. Stir until the sugar is fully dissolved.
    2. Add the raspberry puree to the lemonade mixture. Stir to combine.
    3. If using, stir in the lemon zest and a pinch of salt for added flavor.
3. **Freeze Granita:**
    1. Pour the mixture into a shallow baking dish or pan.
    2. Place the dish in the freezer. Every 30 minutes, use a fork to scrape and stir the mixture to break up ice crystals. Continue this process until the granita is fully frozen and has a fluffy, granular texture. This typically takes about 3-4 hours.
4. **Serve:**
    1. Before serving, use a fork to fluff the granita again.
    2. Scoop into serving glasses or bowls.
    3. Garnish with fresh raspberries or a mint sprig if desired.

Enjoy the refreshing, tangy sweetness of this Raspberry Lemonade Granita—a perfect treat for a hot day!

Salted Caramel Swirl Frozen Yogurt

Ingredients:

For the Salted Caramel Sauce:

- 1 cup granulated sugar
- 6 tablespoons unsalted butter, cut into pieces
- 1/2 cup heavy cream
- 1/2 teaspoon sea salt (adjust to taste)

For the Frozen Yogurt Base:

- 2 cups plain Greek yogurt (full-fat or 2%)
- 1 cup whole milk
- 1/2 cup granulated sugar
- 1 teaspoon vanilla extract

Instructions:

1. **Prepare the Salted Caramel Sauce:**
    1. In a medium saucepan over medium heat, melt the granulated sugar, stirring constantly until it turns a deep amber color.
    2. Carefully add the butter to the melted sugar, stirring until fully combined and smooth.
    3. Gradually add the heavy cream while continuing to stir. Be cautious, as the mixture will bubble vigorously.
    4. Remove from heat and stir in the sea salt. Allow the caramel sauce to cool to room temperature.
2. **Prepare the Frozen Yogurt Base:**
    1. In a medium bowl, whisk together the plain Greek yogurt, whole milk, granulated sugar, and vanilla extract until the sugar is fully dissolved.
3. **Churn the Frozen Yogurt:**
    1. Pour the yogurt mixture into an ice cream maker and churn according to the manufacturer's instructions. This usually takes about 20-25 minutes, or until the yogurt reaches a soft-serve consistency.
4. **Add the Caramel Swirl:**
    1. During the last few minutes of churning, slowly drizzle in about 1/2 cup of the salted caramel sauce while the machine is still running, allowing it to swirl into the frozen yogurt.
5. **Freeze:**
    1. Transfer the churned frozen yogurt to an airtight container.
    2. Drizzle additional salted caramel sauce on top and gently swirl it in with a knife or spatula.
    3. Freeze for at least 2 hours, or until firm.
6. **Serve:**
    1. Scoop and enjoy your Salted Caramel Swirl Frozen Yogurt! For added indulgence, drizzle extra salted caramel sauce on top or garnish with a sprinkle of sea salt.

Relish the creamy, tangy yogurt combined with rich, buttery caramel and a touch of sea salt in this delightful frozen treat!

Blueberry Basil Sorbet

Ingredients:

- 2 cups fresh or frozen blueberries

- 1 cup granulated sugar
- 1 cup water
- 1/2 cup freshly squeezed lemon juice (about 2 lemons)
- 1/4 cup fresh basil leaves, finely chopped
- A pinch of salt

Instructions:

1. **Prepare the Blueberry Mixture:**
   1. In a blender or food processor, combine the blueberries, granulated sugar, and water. Blend until smooth.
   2. Strain the mixture through a fine-mesh sieve into a bowl to remove any skins and seeds.
2. **Add Lemon and Basil:**
   1. Stir the freshly squeezed lemon juice into the blueberry mixture.
   2. Gently fold in the finely chopped basil leaves. Adjust the basil to taste, depending on how pronounced you want the basil flavor to be.
   3. Add a pinch of salt to enhance the flavors and balance the sweetness.
3. **Chill Mixture:**
   1. Cover the mixture and refrigerate for at least 1-2 hours, or until thoroughly chilled.
4. **Freeze Sorbet:**
   1. Pour the chilled mixture into an ice cream maker and churn according to the manufacturer's instructions. This usually takes about 20-25 minutes, or until the sorbet reaches a soft-serve consistency.
5. **Freeze:**
   1. Transfer the churned sorbet to an airtight container.
   2. Freeze for at least 2 hours, or until firm.
6. **Serve:**
   1. Scoop and enjoy your Blueberry Basil Sorbet! Garnish with a few whole blueberries or a small basil leaf if desired.

Savor the refreshing combination of sweet blueberries and aromatic basil in this unique and flavorful sorbet!

Peanut Butter Cup Ice Cream

Ingredients:

For the Ice Cream Base:

- 2 cups whole milk
- 1 cup heavy cream
- 3/4 cup granulated sugar
- 1/2 cup creamy peanut butter
- 1 teaspoon vanilla extract
- A pinch of salt

For the Peanut Butter Swirl:

- 1/2 cup creamy peanut butter
- 1/4 cup granulated sugar
- 1/4 cup whole milk

For the Peanut Butter Cups:

- 1 cup mini peanut butter cups, chopped

Instructions:

1. **Prepare the Ice Cream Base:**
    1. In a medium saucepan, heat the whole milk and heavy cream over medium heat until it begins to steam but does not boil.
    2. In a separate bowl, whisk together the granulated sugar and creamy peanut butter until smooth and well combined.
    3. Gradually add a small amount of the warm milk mixture to the peanut butter mixture to temper it. Stir until smooth.
    4. Return the combined mixture to the saucepan and cook over medium heat, stirring constantly, until the mixture thickens slightly and coats the back of a spoon (about 5-7 minutes). Do not let it boil.
    5. Remove from heat and stir in the vanilla extract and a pinch of salt.
    6. Allow the mixture to cool to room temperature, then cover and refrigerate for at least 2 hours, or until thoroughly chilled.
2. **Prepare the Peanut Butter Swirl:**
    1. In a small bowl, combine the creamy peanut butter, granulated sugar, and whole milk. Stir until smooth and well combined.
3. **Churn the Ice Cream:**
    1. Pour the chilled ice cream base into an ice cream maker and churn according to the manufacturer's instructions. This usually takes about 20-25 minutes, or until the ice cream reaches a soft-serve consistency.
4. **Add Peanut Butter Cups and Swirl:**
    1. During the last few minutes of churning, add the chopped mini peanut butter cups to the ice cream maker.
    2. Transfer the churned ice cream to an airtight container.
    3. Drizzle the peanut butter swirl over the ice cream and gently fold it in with a spatula to create a marble effect.

5. **Freeze:**
    1. Cover and freeze the ice cream for at least 2 hours, or until firm.
6. **Serve:**
    1. Scoop and enjoy your Peanut Butter Cup Ice Cream! For extra indulgence, garnish with additional chopped peanut butter cups if desired.

Delight in the creamy combination of rich peanut butter and chunks of peanut butter cups in this indulgent and satisfying ice cream!

Pina Colada Sorbet

Ingredients:

- 2 cups fresh or canned pineapple chunks

- 1 cup coconut milk (full-fat for a richer flavor)
- 3/4 cup granulated sugar
- 1/2 cup freshly squeezed lime juice (about 2 limes)
- 1/2 teaspoon vanilla extract
- A pinch of salt

Instructions:

1. **Prepare the Pineapple Mixture:**
    1. In a blender or food processor, combine the pineapple chunks, coconut milk, granulated sugar, lime juice, and vanilla extract. Blend until smooth.
    2. Taste the mixture and adjust sweetness or lime juice as needed. Add a pinch of salt to enhance flavors.
2. **Chill the Mixture:**
    1. Cover the pineapple mixture and refrigerate for at least 1-2 hours, or until thoroughly chilled.
3. **Freeze the Sorbet:**
    1. Pour the chilled mixture into an ice cream maker and churn according to the manufacturer's instructions. This typically takes about 20-25 minutes, or until the sorbet reaches a soft-serve consistency.
4. **Freeze:**
    1. Transfer the churned sorbet to an airtight container.
    2. Freeze for at least 2 hours, or until firm.
5. **Serve:**
    1. Scoop and enjoy your refreshing Pina Colada Sorbet! For an extra tropical touch, garnish with a pineapple slice or a cherry if desired.

Enjoy the tropical flavors of pineapple and coconut in this light and refreshing sorbet—perfect for a summer treat or a taste of paradise any time of the year!

Matcha Green Tea Ice Cream

Ingredients:

- 2 cups whole milk
- 1 cup heavy cream
- 3/4 cup granulated sugar
- 3 tablespoons matcha green tea powder (culinary grade)
- 1 teaspoon vanilla extract
- A pinch of salt
- 4 large egg yolks

Instructions:

1. **Prepare the Matcha Mixture:**
    1. In a medium bowl, whisk together the matcha green tea powder and 1/4 cup of the granulated sugar. Add 1/4 cup of whole milk to form a smooth paste. Set aside.
2. **Heat Milk and Cream:**
    1. In a medium saucepan, combine the remaining whole milk and heavy cream. Heat over medium heat until the mixture begins to steam, but do not let it boil.
3. **Whisk Egg Yolks and Sugar:**
    1. In a separate bowl, whisk together the egg yolks and the remaining 1/2 cup of granulated sugar until smooth and pale.
4. **Temper the Egg Yolks:**
    1. Gradually whisk a small amount of the hot milk mixture into the egg yolks to temper them.
    2. Return the egg yolk mixture to the saucepan with the remaining milk mixture.
5. **Cook the Custard Base:**
    1. Cook the mixture over medium heat, stirring constantly, until it thickens slightly and coats the back of a spoon (about 5-7 minutes). Do not let it boil.
6. **Incorporate Matcha:**
    1. Remove the saucepan from heat and stir in the matcha paste until fully combined.
    2. Stir in the vanilla extract and a pinch of salt.
7. **Cool the Custard:**
    1. Pour the custard through a fine-mesh sieve into a clean bowl to remove any lumps.
    2. Allow the mixture to cool to room temperature.
    3. Cover and refrigerate for at least 2 hours, or until thoroughly chilled.
8. **Churn the Ice Cream:**
    1. Pour the chilled mixture into an ice cream maker and churn according to the manufacturer's instructions. This usually takes about 20-25 minutes, or until the ice cream reaches a soft-serve consistency.
9. **Freeze:**
    1. Transfer the churned ice cream to an airtight container.
    2. Freeze for at least 2 hours, or until firm.
10. **Serve:**

1. Scoop and enjoy your Matcha Green Tea Ice Cream! For an extra touch, you can garnish with a sprinkle of matcha powder.

Enjoy the creamy, rich flavor of matcha green tea in this unique and delightful ice cream!

Cookies and Cream Gelato

Ingredients:

For the Gelato Base:

- 2 cups whole milk
- 1 cup heavy cream
- 3/4 cup granulated sugar
- 4 large egg yolks
- 1 teaspoon vanilla extract
- A pinch of salt

For the Cookies and Cream Mix-In:

- 1 1/2 cups chocolate sandwich cookies (e.g., Oreos), coarsely crushed

Instructions:

1. **Prepare the Gelato Base:**
    1. In a medium saucepan, heat the whole milk and heavy cream over medium heat until it begins to steam, but do not let it boil.
    2. In a separate bowl, whisk together the egg yolks and granulated sugar until smooth and pale.
    3. Gradually whisk a small amount of the hot milk mixture into the egg yolks to temper them.
    4. Return the egg yolk mixture to the saucepan with the remaining milk mixture.
2. **Cook the Custard Base:**
    1. Cook the mixture over medium heat, stirring constantly, until it thickens slightly and coats the back of a spoon (about 5-7 minutes). Do not let it boil.
    2. Remove from heat and stir in the vanilla extract and a pinch of salt.
3. **Cool the Custard:**
    1. Pour the custard through a fine-mesh sieve into a clean bowl to remove any lumps.
    2. Allow the mixture to cool to room temperature.
    3. Cover and refrigerate for at least 2 hours, or until thoroughly chilled.
4. **Churn the Gelato:**
    1. Pour the chilled mixture into an ice cream maker and churn according to the manufacturer's instructions. This usually takes about 20-25 minutes, or until the gelato reaches a soft-serve consistency.
5. **Add Cookies and Cream Mix-In:**
    1. During the last few minutes of churning, add the coarsely crushed chocolate sandwich cookies to the gelato maker. Churn until the cookies are evenly distributed throughout the gelato.
6. **Freeze:**
    1. Transfer the churned gelato to an airtight container.
    2. Freeze for at least 2 hours, or until firm.
7. **Serve:**

1. Scoop and enjoy your Cookies and Cream Gelato! For an extra treat, you can garnish with additional cookie crumbs if desired.

Indulge in the creamy, rich texture of gelato with the delightful crunch of cookies in every bite!

Peach Melba Granita

Ingredients:

For the Peach Puree:

- 4 large ripe peaches, peeled and pitted
- 1/4 cup granulated sugar (adjust based on sweetness of peaches)
- 1 tablespoon freshly squeezed lemon juice

For the Raspberry Sauce:

- 1 cup fresh or frozen raspberries
- 1/4 cup granulated sugar
- 1 tablespoon freshly squeezed lemon juice

Instructions:

1. **Prepare the Peach Puree:**
    1. In a blender or food processor, combine the peeled and pitted peaches, granulated sugar, and lemon juice. Blend until smooth.
    2. Taste the mixture and adjust the sweetness with more sugar if needed.
    3. Strain the peach puree through a fine-mesh sieve into a bowl to remove any pulp or fibers.
2. **Prepare the Raspberry Sauce:**
    1. In a small saucepan, combine the raspberries, granulated sugar, and lemon juice. Cook over medium heat, stirring occasionally, until the raspberries break down and the sauce thickens slightly (about 5-7 minutes).
    2. Strain the raspberry sauce through a fine-mesh sieve into a bowl to remove seeds. Allow the sauce to cool to room temperature.
3. **Freeze the Peach Granita:**
    1. Pour the peach puree into a shallow baking dish or pan.
    2. Place the dish in the freezer. Every 30 minutes, use a fork to scrape and stir the mixture to break up ice crystals. Continue this process until the granita is fully frozen and has a fluffy, granular texture. This typically takes about 3-4 hours.
4. **Serve:**
    1. Before serving, use a fork to fluff the granita again.
    2. Scoop the granita into serving glasses or bowls.
    3. Drizzle the raspberry sauce over the top of the peach granita.
    4. Garnish with fresh mint leaves or additional peach slices if desired.

Enjoy the refreshing combination of sweet peaches and tangy raspberries in this light and flavorful granita—perfect for a summer treat!

Mocha Almond Fudge Ice Cream

Ingredients:

For the Ice Cream Base:

- 2 cups whole milk
- 1 cup heavy cream
- 3/4 cup granulated sugar
- 1/2 cup unsweetened cocoa powder
- 1/2 cup strong brewed coffee, cooled
- 1 teaspoon vanilla extract
- A pinch of salt

For the Fudge Swirl:

- 1/2 cup semi-sweet chocolate chips
- 1/4 cup heavy cream
- 1 tablespoon light corn syrup (optional, for smoother consistency)

For the Almonds:

- 1/2 cup toasted almonds, chopped

Instructions:

1. **Prepare the Ice Cream Base:**
    1. In a medium saucepan, combine the whole milk, heavy cream, granulated sugar, and cocoa powder.
    2. Heat over medium heat, stirring constantly, until the mixture is warm and the sugar and cocoa powder are fully dissolved. Do not let it boil.
    3. Stir in the cooled brewed coffee, vanilla extract, and a pinch of salt.
    4. Remove from heat and allow the mixture to cool to room temperature.
    5. Cover and refrigerate for at least 2 hours, or until thoroughly chilled.
2. **Prepare the Fudge Swirl:**
    1. In a small saucepan over low heat, combine the semi-sweet chocolate chips, heavy cream, and light corn syrup (if using). Stir until smooth and fully melted.
    2. Remove from heat and let the fudge sauce cool slightly. It should be pourable but not too hot.
3. **Churn the Ice Cream:**
    1. Pour the chilled ice cream base into an ice cream maker and churn according to the manufacturer's instructions. This usually takes about 20-25 minutes, or until the ice cream reaches a soft-serve consistency.
    2. During the last few minutes of churning, add the toasted chopped almonds to the ice cream maker.
4. **Add Fudge Swirl:**
    1. Transfer the churned ice cream to an airtight container.

2. Drizzle the fudge sauce over the top and gently swirl it into the ice cream with a spatula or knife. Be careful not to overmix; you want to achieve a marbled effect.
5. **Freeze:**
    1. Cover the container and freeze the ice cream for at least 2 hours, or until firm.
6. **Serve:**
    1. Scoop and enjoy your Mocha Almond Fudge Ice Cream! For an extra touch, garnish with additional chopped almonds or a drizzle of fudge sauce if desired.

Indulge in the rich flavors of mocha combined with crunchy almonds and creamy fudge in this delectable ice cream!

Pineapple Coconut Frozen Smoothie

Ingredients:

- 2 cups fresh or frozen pineapple chunks
- 1 cup coconut milk (full-fat for a creamier texture)
- 1/2 cup Greek yogurt (plain or vanilla)
- 1 banana, peeled and sliced
- 2 tablespoons honey or agave syrup (adjust to taste)
- 1/2 cup ice cubes (if using fresh pineapple)
- A pinch of salt
- Optional: 1 tablespoon shredded coconut for garnish

Instructions:

1. **Blend the Ingredients:**
    1. In a blender, combine the pineapple chunks, coconut milk, Greek yogurt, banana, and honey.
    2. Add the ice cubes if you're using fresh pineapple to make the smoothie cold and frothy.
    3. Blend on high until smooth and creamy. If the smoothie is too thick, you can add a bit more coconut milk or water to reach your desired consistency.
2. **Adjust Sweetness:**
    1. Taste the smoothie and adjust the sweetness with more honey or agave syrup if needed.
3. **Serve:**
    1. Pour the smoothie into glasses.
    2. Garnish with shredded coconut on top if desired.

Enjoy your tropical Pineapple Coconut Frozen Smoothie, a refreshing blend of sweet pineapple, creamy coconut, and a hint of banana—perfect for a quick breakfast or a cool afternoon treat!

Raspberry White Chocolate Gelato

Ingredients:

For the Raspberry Puree:

- 2 cups fresh or frozen raspberries
- 1/4 cup granulated sugar
- 1 tablespoon freshly squeezed lemon juice

For the Gelato Base:

- 2 cups whole milk
- 1 cup heavy cream
- 3/4 cup granulated sugar
- 4 ounces white chocolate, finely chopped
- 1 teaspoon vanilla extract
- A pinch of salt
- 4 large egg yolks

Instructions:

1. **Prepare the Raspberry Puree:**
    1. In a blender or food processor, combine the raspberries, granulated sugar, and lemon juice. Blend until smooth.
    2. Strain the raspberry puree through a fine-mesh sieve into a bowl to remove seeds. Set aside.
2. **Prepare the Gelato Base:**
    1. In a medium saucepan, heat the whole milk and heavy cream over medium heat until it begins to steam, but do not let it boil.
    2. In a separate bowl, whisk together the egg yolks and granulated sugar until smooth and pale.
    3. Gradually whisk a small amount of the hot milk mixture into the egg yolks to temper them.
    4. Return the egg yolk mixture to the saucepan with the remaining milk mixture.
    5. Cook over medium heat, stirring constantly, until the mixture thickens slightly and coats the back of a spoon (about 5-7 minutes). Do not let it boil.
3. **Incorporate White Chocolate:**
    1. Remove from heat and stir in the finely chopped white chocolate until fully melted and smooth.
    2. Stir in the vanilla extract and a pinch of salt.
4. **Cool the Custard:**
    1. Pour the custard through a fine-mesh sieve into a clean bowl to remove any lumps.
    2. Allow the mixture to cool to room temperature.
    3. Cover and refrigerate for at least 2 hours, or until thoroughly chilled.
5. **Churn the Gelato:**

1. Pour the chilled mixture into an ice cream maker and churn according to the manufacturer's instructions. This usually takes about 20-25 minutes, or until the gelato reaches a soft-serve consistency.
6. **Add Raspberry Swirl:**
    1. During the last few minutes of churning, gently fold in the raspberry puree. You can swirl it in lightly to create a marbled effect.
7. **Freeze:**
    1. Transfer the churned gelato to an airtight container.
    2. Freeze for at least 2 hours, or until firm.
8. **Serve:**
    1. Scoop and enjoy your Raspberry White Chocolate Gelato! For an extra touch, garnish with fresh raspberries or a drizzle of raspberry sauce if desired.

Enjoy the creamy blend of sweet white chocolate with a tangy raspberry swirl in this luxurious gelato!

Lemon Basil Sorbet

Ingredients:

- 1 cup fresh basil leaves, packed
- 1 cup freshly squeezed lemon juice (about 4-5 lemons)
- 1 1/2 cups granulated sugar
- 1 1/2 cups water
- 1 tablespoon lemon zest (optional, for extra flavor)
- A pinch of salt

Instructions:

1. **Prepare the Basil Infusion:**
    1. In a small saucepan, bring 1 cup of water to a boil.
    2. Remove from heat and add the fresh basil leaves.
    3. Cover and steep for about 10 minutes to infuse the basil flavor into the water.
    4. Strain the basil leaves from the water and discard the leaves. Allow the basil-infused water to cool.
2. **Prepare the Lemon Mixture:**
    1. In a large bowl, combine the lemon juice, granulated sugar, and the remaining 1/2 cup of water. Stir until the sugar is fully dissolved.
    2. Stir in the cooled basil-infused water and a pinch of salt. If using, add the lemon zest for extra citrus flavor.
3. **Chill the Mixture:**
    1. Cover the mixture and refrigerate for at least 1-2 hours, or until thoroughly chilled.
4. **Freeze the Sorbet:**
    1. Pour the chilled mixture into an ice cream maker and churn according to the manufacturer's instructions. This typically takes about 20-25 minutes, or until the sorbet reaches a soft-serve consistency.
5. **Freeze:**
    1. Transfer the churned sorbet to an airtight container.
    2. Freeze for at least 2 hours, or until firm.
6. **Serve:**
    1. Scoop and enjoy your Lemon Basil Sorbet! For an elegant touch, garnish with fresh basil leaves or a lemon twist if desired.

Enjoy the refreshing combination of zesty lemon and aromatic basil in this light and delightful sorbet!

Hazelnut Coffee Ice Cream

Ingredients:

For the Ice Cream Base:

- 2 cups whole milk
- 1 cup heavy cream
- 3/4 cup granulated sugar
- 1/2 cup ground hazelnuts
- 1/2 cup brewed strong coffee (cooled)
- 1 teaspoon vanilla extract
- A pinch of salt
- 4 large egg yolks

For the Hazelnut Swirl (Optional):

- 1/2 cup hazelnut spread (like Nutella)

Instructions:

1. **Infuse the Milk:**
    1. In a medium saucepan, combine the whole milk and heavy cream. Heat over medium heat until the mixture begins to steam but does not boil.
    2. Stir in the ground hazelnuts and cook for 5-7 minutes to infuse the hazelnut flavor into the milk mixture. Remove from heat and let it steep for an additional 10 minutes.
2. **Prepare the Egg Yolk Mixture:**
    1. In a separate bowl, whisk together the egg yolks and granulated sugar until smooth and pale.
3. **Temper the Egg Yolks:**
    1. Gradually whisk a small amount of the hot milk mixture into the egg yolks to temper them.
    2. Return the egg yolk mixture to the saucepan with the remaining milk mixture.
4. **Cook the Custard Base:**
    1. Cook the mixture over medium heat, stirring constantly, until it thickens slightly and coats the back of a spoon (about 5-7 minutes). Do not let it boil.
    2. Remove from heat and stir in the cooled brewed coffee, vanilla extract, and a pinch of salt.
5. **Cool the Custard:**
    1. Pour the custard through a fine-mesh sieve into a clean bowl to remove any hazelnut particles or lumps.
    2. Allow the mixture to cool to room temperature.
    3. Cover and refrigerate for at least 2 hours, or until thoroughly chilled.
6. **Churn the Ice Cream:**

1. Pour the chilled mixture into an ice cream maker and churn according to the manufacturer's instructions. This usually takes about 20-25 minutes, or until the ice cream reaches a soft-serve consistency.
7. **Add Hazelnut Swirl (Optional):**
    1. If using hazelnut spread, gently swirl it into the churned ice cream during the last few minutes of churning or fold it in after churning.
8. **Freeze:**
    1. Transfer the churned ice cream to an airtight container.
    2. Freeze for at least 2 hours, or until firm.
9. **Serve:**
    1. Scoop and enjoy your Hazelnut Coffee Ice Cream! For an extra touch, you can garnish with chopped toasted hazelnuts or a drizzle of additional hazelnut spread if desired.

Indulge in the rich flavors of hazelnut and coffee in this creamy, luxurious ice cream that's perfect for any time you need a decadent treat!

Blackberry Mint Frozen Yogurt

Ingredients:

For the Blackberry Puree:

- 2 cups fresh or frozen blackberries
- 1/4 cup granulated sugar (adjust to taste)
- 1 tablespoon freshly squeezed lemon juice

For the Frozen Yogurt Base:

- 2 cups plain Greek yogurt (full-fat or 2% for creamier texture)
- 1 cup heavy cream
- 1/2 cup granulated sugar
- 1 teaspoon vanilla extract
- 1/2 cup fresh mint leaves, finely chopped
- A pinch of salt

Instructions:

1. **Prepare the Blackberry Puree:**
    1. In a blender or food processor, combine the blackberries, granulated sugar, and lemon juice. Blend until smooth.
    2. Strain the blackberry puree through a fine-mesh sieve into a bowl to remove seeds. Set aside.
2. **Prepare the Frozen Yogurt Base:**
    1. In a large bowl, whisk together the Greek yogurt, heavy cream, granulated sugar, and vanilla extract until the sugar is fully dissolved and the mixture is smooth.
    2. Stir in the finely chopped fresh mint leaves and a pinch of salt.
3. **Combine Blackberry Puree:**
    1. Gently fold the blackberry puree into the yogurt mixture. You can swirl it in lightly to create a marbled effect or fully combine it for a uniform color.
4. **Chill the Mixture:**
    1. Cover the mixture and refrigerate for at least 1-2 hours, or until thoroughly chilled.
5. **Freeze the Yogurt:**
    1. Pour the chilled mixture into an ice cream maker and churn according to the manufacturer's instructions. This typically takes about 20-25 minutes, or until the frozen yogurt reaches a soft-serve consistency.
6. **Freeze:**
    1. Transfer the churned frozen yogurt to an airtight container.
    2. Freeze for at least 2 hours, or until firm.
7. **Serve:**
    1. Scoop and enjoy your Blackberry Mint Frozen Yogurt! For an extra touch, garnish with fresh mint leaves or a few additional blackberry halves if desired.

Enjoy the refreshing blend of sweet blackberries and cool mint in this creamy, tangy frozen yogurt—perfect for a light and delicious dessert!

Cinnamon Roll Ice Cream

Ingredients:

For the Ice Cream Base:

- 2 cups whole milk
- 1 cup heavy cream
- 3/4 cup granulated sugar
- 1 teaspoon vanilla extract
- 1 teaspoon ground cinnamon
- A pinch of salt
- 4 large egg yolks

For the Cinnamon Swirl:

- 1/2 cup brown sugar
- 1 tablespoon ground cinnamon
- 2 tablespoons unsalted butter
- 1/4 cup heavy cream
- 1/4 teaspoon vanilla extract

For the Optional Add-ins:

- 1/2 cup chopped cinnamon rolls or cinnamon roll pieces (store-bought or homemade)

Instructions:

1. **Prepare the Ice Cream Base:**
    1. In a medium saucepan, heat the whole milk and heavy cream over medium heat until it begins to steam but does not boil.
    2. In a separate bowl, whisk together the egg yolks, granulated sugar, ground cinnamon, and a pinch of salt until smooth.
    3. Gradually whisk a small amount of the hot milk mixture into the egg yolks to temper them.
    4. Return the egg yolk mixture to the saucepan with the remaining milk mixture.
    5. Cook over medium heat, stirring constantly, until the mixture thickens slightly and coats the back of a spoon (about 5-7 minutes). Do not let it boil.
2. **Cool the Custard Base:**
    1. Remove from heat and stir in the vanilla extract.
    2. Pour the custard through a fine-mesh sieve into a clean bowl to remove any lumps.
    3. Allow the mixture to cool to room temperature.
    4. Cover and refrigerate for at least 2 hours, or until thoroughly chilled.
3. **Prepare the Cinnamon Swirl:**
    1. In a small saucepan, melt the unsalted butter over medium heat.
    2. Stir in the brown sugar and ground cinnamon, and cook until the sugar is dissolved and the mixture is smooth (about 2-3 minutes).

3. Remove from heat and stir in the heavy cream and vanilla extract. Allow the cinnamon swirl to cool to room temperature.
4. **Churn the Ice Cream:**
    1. Pour the chilled ice cream base into an ice cream maker and churn according to the manufacturer's instructions. This typically takes about 20-25 minutes, or until the ice cream reaches a soft-serve consistency.
5. **Add Cinnamon Roll Pieces:**
    1. If using, gently fold in the chopped cinnamon roll pieces during the last few minutes of churning.
6. **Add Cinnamon Swirl:**
    1. Transfer the churned ice cream to an airtight container.
    2. Drizzle the cooled cinnamon swirl over the top and gently swirl it into the ice cream with a spatula or knife. Be careful not to overmix; you want a marbled effect.
7. **Freeze:**
    1. Cover the container and freeze the ice cream for at least 2 hours, or until firm.
8. **Serve:**
    1. Scoop and enjoy your Cinnamon Roll Ice Cream! For an extra touch, you can garnish with additional cinnamon roll pieces or a drizzle of the cinnamon swirl sauce if desired.

Indulge in the creamy, comforting flavors of cinnamon roll in this delightful ice cream, combining the warmth of cinnamon with a rich, creamy bas

Watermelon Mint Granita

Ingredients:

- 4 cups seedless watermelon, cut into chunks
- 1/4 cup freshly squeezed lime juice (about 2 limes)
- 1/4 cup granulated sugar (adjust to taste)
- 1/4 cup fresh mint leaves
- 1/2 cup water
- A pinch of salt

Instructions:

1. **Prepare the Watermelon Mixture:**
    1. In a blender or food processor, combine the watermelon chunks, freshly squeezed lime juice, granulated sugar, and a pinch of salt.
    2. Blend until smooth.
2. **Infuse with Mint:**
    1. In a small saucepan, heat 1/2 cup water until warm (not boiling).
    2. Add the fresh mint leaves and steep for about 5 minutes to infuse the mint flavor.
    3. Strain the mint leaves from the water and discard the leaves. Allow the mint-infused water to cool.
3. **Combine and Chill:**
    1. Stir the cooled mint-infused water into the watermelon mixture.
    2. Pour the mixture into a shallow baking dish or pan.
4. **Freeze and Scrape:**
    1. Place the dish in the freezer.
    2. Every 30 minutes, use a fork to scrape and stir the mixture, breaking up any ice crystals that form. Continue this process until the granita is fully frozen and has a fluffy, granular texture. This typically takes about 3-4 hours.
5. **Serve:**
    1. Before serving, use a fork to fluff the granita again.
    2. Scoop the granita into glasses or bowls.
    3. Garnish with additional mint leaves if desired.

Enjoy the refreshing and light combination of sweet watermelon and cool mint in this easy-to-make granita—perfect for a hot day or as a palate cleanser!

Pumpkin Spice Frozen Custard

Ingredients:

For the Custard Base:

- 2 cups whole milk
- 1 cup heavy cream
- 3/4 cup granulated sugar
- 4 large egg yolks
- 1 cup pumpkin puree (canned or homemade)
- 1 teaspoon pumpkin pie spice (or a mix of ground cinnamon, ginger, nutmeg, and cloves)
- 1/2 teaspoon vanilla extract
- A pinch of salt

Instructions:

1. **Prepare the Custard Base:**
    1. In a medium saucepan, combine the whole milk and heavy cream. Heat over medium heat until the mixture begins to steam, but do not let it boil.
    2. In a separate bowl, whisk together the egg yolks and granulated sugar until smooth and pale.
    3. Gradually whisk a small amount of the hot milk mixture into the egg yolks to temper them.
    4. Return the egg yolk mixture to the saucepan with the remaining milk mixture.
    5. Cook over medium heat, stirring constantly, until the mixture thickens slightly and coats the back of a spoon (about 5-7 minutes). Do not let it boil.
2. **Incorporate Pumpkin and Spices:**
    1. Remove from heat and stir in the pumpkin puree, pumpkin pie spice, vanilla extract, and a pinch of salt.
    2. Pour the custard through a fine-mesh sieve into a clean bowl to remove any lumps.
    3. Allow the mixture to cool to room temperature.
3. **Chill the Mixture:**
    1. Cover the bowl with plastic wrap and refrigerate for at least 2 hours, or until thoroughly chilled.
4. **Churn the Custard:**
    1. Pour the chilled custard mixture into an ice cream maker and churn according to the manufacturer's instructions. This typically takes about 20-25 minutes, or until the custard reaches a soft-serve consistency.
5. **Freeze:**
    1. Transfer the churned custard to an airtight container.
    2. Freeze for at least 2 hours, or until firm.
6. **Serve:**
    1. Scoop and enjoy your Pumpkin Spice Frozen Custard! For an extra touch, you can garnish with a sprinkle of cinnamon or a dollop of whipped cream.

Enjoy the creamy, spiced flavor of pumpkin pie in this rich and indulgent frozen custard, perfect for autumn or anytime you crave a seasonal treat!

Chocolate Raspberry Sorbet

Ingredients:

- 2 cups fresh or frozen raspberries
- 1 cup granulated sugar
- 1/2 cup water
- 1/2 cup unsweetened cocoa powder
- 1 tablespoon lemon juice (optional, for a bit of brightness)
- A pinch of salt

Instructions:

1. **Prepare the Raspberry Puree:**
   1. In a blender or food processor, blend the raspberries until smooth.
   2. Strain the raspberry puree through a fine-mesh sieve into a bowl to remove the seeds. Set aside.
2. **Prepare the Chocolate Base:**
   1. In a small saucepan, combine the water and granulated sugar. Heat over medium heat, stirring occasionally, until the sugar is fully dissolved and the mixture is clear.
   2. Remove from heat and whisk in the unsweetened cocoa powder until smooth and fully incorporated.
   3. Stir in the lemon juice (if using) and a pinch of salt. Allow the chocolate mixture to cool to room temperature.
3. **Combine Raspberry and Chocolate:**
   1. Mix the cooled chocolate base into the raspberry puree until well combined.
4. **Chill the Mixture:**
   1. Cover the mixture and refrigerate for at least 1-2 hours, or until thoroughly chilled.
5. **Freeze the Sorbet:**
   1. Pour the chilled mixture into an ice cream maker and churn according to the manufacturer's instructions. This typically takes about 20-25 minutes, or until the sorbet reaches a soft-serve consistency.
6. **Freeze:**
   1. Transfer the churned sorbet to an airtight container.
   2. Freeze for at least 2 hours, or until firm.
7. **Serve:**
   1. Scoop and enjoy your Chocolate Raspberry Sorbet! For an extra touch, you can garnish with fresh raspberries or a sprinkle of shaved chocolate.

Indulge in the rich, tangy-sweet blend of raspberry and chocolate in this refreshing sorbet, perfect for a sophisticated dessert or a cool summer treat!

Almond Joy Gelato

Ingredients:

For the Gelato Base:

- 2 cups whole milk
- 1 cup heavy cream
- 3/4 cup granulated sugar
- 1 teaspoon vanilla extract
- 1/2 cup sweetened shredded coconut
- 1/2 cup chopped almonds
- 1/2 cup mini chocolate chips or chopped dark chocolate
- 4 large egg yolks
- A pinch of salt

For the Almond Swirl (Optional):

- 1/4 cup almond butter or hazelnut spread
- 2 tablespoons granulated sugar

Instructions:

1. **Prepare the Gelato Base:**
    1. In a medium saucepan, combine the whole milk and heavy cream. Heat over medium heat until the mixture begins to steam, but do not let it boil.
    2. In a separate bowl, whisk together the egg yolks and granulated sugar until smooth and pale.
    3. Gradually whisk a small amount of the hot milk mixture into the egg yolks to temper them.
    4. Return the egg yolk mixture to the saucepan with the remaining milk mixture.
    5. Cook over medium heat, stirring constantly, until the mixture thickens slightly and coats the back of a spoon (about 5-7 minutes). Do not let it boil.
2. **Cool the Custard Base:**
    1. Remove from heat and stir in the vanilla extract and a pinch of salt.
    2. Pour the custard through a fine-mesh sieve into a clean bowl to remove any lumps.
    3. Stir in the shredded coconut and allow the mixture to cool to room temperature.
    4. Cover and refrigerate for at least 2 hours, or until thoroughly chilled.
3. **Prepare the Almond Swirl (Optional):**
    1. In a small bowl, combine the almond butter or hazelnut spread with the granulated sugar. Mix until smooth and set aside.
4. **Churn the Gelato:**
    1. Pour the chilled custard mixture into an ice cream maker and churn according to the manufacturer's instructions. This typically takes about 20-25 minutes, or until the gelato reaches a soft-serve consistency.
    2. During the last few minutes of churning, gently fold in the chopped almonds and mini chocolate chips.
5. **Add Almond Swirl (Optional):**

        1. If using the almond swirl, transfer half of the churned gelato to an airtight container.
        2. Drizzle a portion of the almond mixture over the gelato.
        3. Add the remaining gelato on top and gently swirl with a knife or spatula to create a marbled effect.
6. **Freeze:**
        1. Cover the container and freeze for at least 2 hours, or until firm.
7. **Serve:**
        1. Scoop and enjoy your Almond Joy Gelato! For an extra touch, you can garnish with additional chopped almonds or a sprinkle of shredded coconut.

Indulge in the creamy, nutty, and chocolatey flavors of this gelato, reminiscent of the classic Almond Joy candy bar, but with a sophisticated gelato twist!

Key Lime Pie Frozen Yogurt

Ingredients:

For the Yogurt Base:

- 2 cups plain Greek yogurt (full-fat or 2% for creamier texture)
- 1 cup heavy cream
- 1/2 cup granulated sugar
- 1/2 cup freshly squeezed key lime juice (about 4-6 key limes)
- 1 tablespoon key lime zest
- 1 teaspoon vanilla extract
- A pinch of salt

For the Graham Cracker Swirl:

- 1 cup graham cracker crumbs
- 1/4 cup granulated sugar
- 3 tablespoons unsalted butter, melted

Instructions:

1. **Prepare the Yogurt Base:**
    1. In a large bowl, whisk together the Greek yogurt, heavy cream, granulated sugar, key lime juice, key lime zest, vanilla extract, and a pinch of salt until smooth and the sugar is fully dissolved.
2. **Chill the Mixture:**
    1. Cover the mixture and refrigerate for at least 1-2 hours, or until thoroughly chilled.
3. **Prepare the Graham Cracker Swirl:**
    1. In a medium bowl, combine the graham cracker crumbs, granulated sugar, and melted butter. Mix until the crumbs are well-coated and slightly clumped together.
4. **Churn the Frozen Yogurt:**
    1. Pour the chilled yogurt mixture into an ice cream maker and churn according to the manufacturer's instructions. This typically takes about 20-25 minutes, or until the yogurt reaches a soft-serve consistency.
5. **Add Graham Cracker Swirl:**
    1. During the last few minutes of churning, gently fold in the graham cracker crumb mixture. You want to swirl the crumbs into the yogurt, not fully mix them in, to create pockets of graham cracker crust.
6. **Freeze:**
    1. Transfer the churned frozen yogurt to an airtight container.
    2. Freeze for at least 2 hours, or until firm.
7. **Serve:**
    1. Scoop and enjoy your Key Lime Pie Frozen Yogurt! For an extra touch, garnish with additional graham cracker crumbs or a slice of lime.

Experience the tangy, creamy flavor of classic key lime pie in this refreshing frozen yogurt, complete with a delightful graham cracker swirl!

Espresso Affogato

Ingredients:

- 2 cups vanilla ice cream or gelato
- 1 cup freshly brewed espresso (hot)
- 2 tablespoons sugar (optional, to sweeten the espresso)
- Whipped cream (optional, for garnish)

- Cocoa powder or chocolate shavings (optional, for garnish)

Instructions:

1. **Brew the Espresso:**
    1. Brew a cup of strong espresso. If you prefer a sweeter espresso, stir in 2 tablespoons of sugar while the coffee is still hot. Let it cool slightly.
2. **Scoop the Ice Cream:**
    1. Place 1-2 scoops of vanilla ice cream or gelato into each serving glass or bowl.
3. **Pour the Espresso:**
    1. Pour the hot espresso directly over the ice cream.
4. **Garnish (Optional):**
    1. Top with a dollop of whipped cream, if desired.
    2. Sprinkle with cocoa powder or chocolate shavings for an extra touch of indulgence.
5. **Serve Immediately:**
    1. Serve the affogato immediately, while the espresso is still hot and the ice cream is starting to melt.

Enjoy the classic Italian treat that combines the rich bitterness of espresso with the creamy sweetness of vanilla ice cream—a perfect balance of flavors and temperatures!

Cherry Vanilla Ice Cream

Ingredients:

For the Ice Cream Base:

- 2 cups whole milk
- 1 cup heavy cream
- 3/4 cup granulated sugar
- 1 tablespoon vanilla extract
- A pinch of salt
- 4 large egg yolks

For the Cherry Swirl:

- 2 cups fresh or frozen cherries, pitted and halved
- 1/4 cup granulated sugar
- 1 tablespoon freshly squeezed lemon juice
- 1/2 teaspoon vanilla extract

Instructions:

1. **Prepare the Cherry Swirl:**
    1. In a medium saucepan, combine the cherries, granulated sugar, and lemon juice.

2. Cook over medium heat, stirring occasionally, until the cherries are softened and the mixture has thickened slightly (about 10-15 minutes).
3. Remove from heat and stir in the vanilla extract.
4. Let the cherry mixture cool to room temperature, then transfer to a bowl and refrigerate until chilled.

2. **Prepare the Ice Cream Base:**
    1. In a medium saucepan, combine the whole milk and heavy cream. Heat over medium heat until the mixture begins to steam, but do not let it boil.
    2. In a separate bowl, whisk together the egg yolks and granulated sugar until smooth and pale.
    3. Gradually whisk a small amount of the hot milk mixture into the egg yolks to temper them.
    4. Return the egg yolk mixture to the saucepan with the remaining milk mixture.
    5. Cook over medium heat, stirring constantly, until the mixture thickens slightly and coats the back of a spoon (about 5-7 minutes). Do not let it boil.
3. **Cool the Custard Base:**
    1. Remove from heat and stir in the vanilla extract and a pinch of salt.
    2. Pour the custard through a fine-mesh sieve into a clean bowl to remove any lumps.
    3. Allow the mixture to cool to room temperature.
    4. Cover and refrigerate for at least 2 hours, or until thoroughly chilled.
4. **Churn the Ice Cream:**
    1. Pour the chilled custard mixture into an ice cream maker and churn according to the manufacturer's instructions. This typically takes about 20-25 minutes, or until the ice cream reaches a soft-serve consistency.
5. **Add Cherry Swirl:**
    1. During the last few minutes of churning, gently fold in the chilled cherry mixture. You can swirl it in lightly or fold it in for a more uniform mix.
6. **Freeze:**
    1. Transfer the churned ice cream to an airtight container.
    2. Freeze for at least 2 hours, or until firm.
7. **Serve:**
    1. Scoop and enjoy your Cherry Vanilla Ice Cream! For an extra touch, garnish with additional fresh cherries or a drizzle of cherry sauce if desired.

Savor the classic combination of rich vanilla ice cream and sweet, tart cherries in this deliciously creamy treat!

Tropical Fruit Sorbet

Ingredients:

- 2 cups fresh or frozen tropical fruits (such as mango, pineapple, and papaya, or a mix)
- 1 cup granulated sugar (adjust to taste)
- 1/2 cup freshly squeezed lime juice (about 3-4 limes)

- 1/2 cup water
- 1/4 teaspoon salt
- 1 teaspoon vanilla extract (optional)

Instructions:

1. **Prepare the Fruit Puree:**
    1. In a blender or food processor, combine the tropical fruits and water. Blend until smooth.
    2. Taste and adjust sweetness by adding granulated sugar, a little at a time, until the mixture reaches your desired level of sweetness. Blend again to combine.
2. **Add Lime Juice and Salt:**
    1. Stir in the freshly squeezed lime juice and a pinch of salt. If using, add the vanilla extract and blend to incorporate.
3. **Chill the Mixture:**
    1. Transfer the mixture to a bowl or pitcher and refrigerate for at least 1-2 hours, or until thoroughly chilled.
4. **Freeze the Sorbet:**
    1. Pour the chilled mixture into an ice cream maker and churn according to the manufacturer's instructions. This typically takes about 20-25 minutes, or until the sorbet reaches a soft-serve consistency.
5. **Freeze:**
    1. Transfer the churned sorbet to an airtight container.
    2. Freeze for at least 2 hours, or until firm.
6. **Serve:**
    1. Scoop and enjoy your Tropical Fruit Sorbet! For an extra touch, garnish with fresh mint leaves or a slice of lime.

Enjoy the refreshing and vibrant flavors of tropical fruits in this light and fruity sorbet, perfect for a cool and exotic treat!

Nutella Swirl Gelato

Ingredients:

For the Gelato Base:

- 2 cups whole milk

- 1 cup heavy cream
- 3/4 cup granulated sugar
- 4 large egg yolks
- 1 teaspoon vanilla extract
- A pinch of salt

For the Nutella Swirl:

- 1/2 cup Nutella (or other hazelnut chocolate spread)

Instructions:

1. **Prepare the Gelato Base:**
    1. In a medium saucepan, combine the whole milk and heavy cream. Heat over medium heat until it begins to steam but does not boil.
    2. In a separate bowl, whisk together the egg yolks and granulated sugar until smooth and pale.
    3. Gradually whisk a small amount of the hot milk mixture into the egg yolks to temper them.
    4. Return the egg yolk mixture to the saucepan with the remaining milk mixture.
    5. Cook over medium heat, stirring constantly, until the mixture thickens slightly and coats the back of a spoon (about 5-7 minutes). Do not let it boil.
2. **Cool the Custard Base:**
    1. Remove from heat and stir in the vanilla extract and a pinch of salt.
    2. Pour the custard through a fine-mesh sieve into a clean bowl to remove any lumps.
    3. Allow the mixture to cool to room temperature.
    4. Cover and refrigerate for at least 2 hours, or until thoroughly chilled.
3. **Churn the Gelato:**
    1. Pour the chilled custard mixture into an ice cream maker and churn according to the manufacturer's instructions. This typically takes about 20-25 minutes, or until the gelato reaches a soft-serve consistency.
4. **Add Nutella Swirl:**
    1. Gently heat the Nutella in the microwave or over a double boiler to make it easier to swirl.
    2. Transfer the churned gelato to an airtight container.
    3. Drizzle the warmed Nutella over the top of the gelato.
    4. Use a knife or spatula to gently swirl the Nutella into the gelato. Be careful not to overmix; you want a marbled effect.
5. **Freeze:**
    1. Cover the container and freeze for at least 2 hours, or until firm.
6. **Serve:**
    1. Scoop and enjoy your Nutella Swirl Gelato! For an extra touch, you can garnish with additional Nutella or chopped hazelnuts.

Indulge in the rich, creamy gelato with swirls of decadent Nutella, blending the smoothness of gelato with the irresistible flavor of hazelnut chocolate!

Spiced Apple Frozen Smoothie

Ingredients:

- 2 cups frozen apple chunks (or fresh apple chunks, frozen)
- 1 cup apple juice or cider
- 1/2 cup plain Greek yogurt

- 1 banana, peeled and frozen
- 1/2 teaspoon ground cinnamon
- 1/4 teaspoon ground nutmeg
- 1/4 teaspoon ground ginger
- 1 tablespoon honey or maple syrup (optional, for added sweetness)
- 1/2 cup ice cubes (optional, if you want a thicker consistency)

Instructions:

1. **Blend the Ingredients:**
    1. In a blender, combine the frozen apple chunks, apple juice or cider, Greek yogurt, and frozen banana.
    2. Add the ground cinnamon, nutmeg, and ginger. Blend until smooth.
2. **Adjust Sweetness:**
    1. Taste the smoothie and add honey or maple syrup if needed for additional sweetness. Blend again to incorporate.
3. **Add Ice (Optional):**
    1. If you prefer a thicker smoothie, add the ice cubes and blend until smooth.
4. **Serve:**
    1. Pour the smoothie into glasses.
    2. Garnish with a sprinkle of cinnamon or a slice of apple, if desired.

Enjoy the comforting, spiced flavors of apple pie in a refreshing frozen smoothie, perfect for a healthy snack or a light dessert!

Hibiscus Raspberry Sorbet

Ingredients:

- 2 cups fresh or frozen raspberries
- 1/2 cup dried hibiscus flowers
- 1 cup granulated sugar

- 1 cup water
- 1/2 cup freshly squeezed lemon juice (about 2-3 lemons)
- 1/2 teaspoon vanilla extract (optional)
- A pinch of salt

Instructions:

1. **Prepare the Hibiscus Tea:**
    1. In a medium saucepan, bring 1 cup of water to a boil.
    2. Remove from heat and add the dried hibiscus flowers.
    3. Let the flowers steep for about 10 minutes, then strain the liquid through a fine-mesh sieve into a bowl. Discard the flowers and set the hibiscus tea aside to cool.
2. **Prepare the Raspberry Puree:**
    1. In a blender or food processor, blend the raspberries until smooth.
    2. Strain the raspberry puree through a fine-mesh sieve to remove the seeds. Set aside.
3. **Make the Sorbet Base:**
    1. In a medium saucepan, combine the granulated sugar and 1 cup of water. Heat over medium heat, stirring occasionally, until the sugar is completely dissolved. Allow the syrup to cool to room temperature.
    2. Stir the cooled hibiscus tea into the sugar syrup.
4. **Combine Ingredients:**
    1. Mix the raspberry puree, hibiscus syrup, freshly squeezed lemon juice, and a pinch of salt in a bowl. Stir until well combined.
    2. If using, add the vanilla extract and mix thoroughly.
5. **Chill the Mixture:**
    1. Cover the mixture and refrigerate for at least 1-2 hours, or until thoroughly chilled.
6. **Freeze the Sorbet:**
    1. Pour the chilled mixture into an ice cream maker and churn according to the manufacturer's instructions. This typically takes about 20-25 minutes, or until the sorbet reaches a soft-serve consistency.
7. **Freeze:**
    1. Transfer the churned sorbet to an airtight container.
    2. Freeze for at least 2 hours, or until firm.
8. **Serve:**
    1. Scoop and enjoy your Hibiscus Raspberry Sorbet! Garnish with fresh raspberries or a mint sprig, if desired.

Delight in the floral and fruity combination of hibiscus and raspberry in this refreshing sorbet, perfect for a light and exotic dessert!

Caramel Macchiato Ice Cream

Ingredients:

For the Ice Cream Base:

- 2 cups whole milk
- 1 cup heavy cream
- 3/4 cup granulated sugar
- 1 tablespoon vanilla extract

- 1 tablespoon instant coffee or espresso powder
- A pinch of salt
- 4 large egg yolks

For the Caramel Swirl:

- 1/2 cup caramel sauce (store-bought or homemade)
- 1 tablespoon sea salt (optional, for salted caramel)

Instructions:

1. **Prepare the Caramel Sauce (If Homemade):**
    1. In a medium saucepan, cook 1 cup granulated sugar over medium heat, stirring constantly, until it melts and turns a deep amber color.
    2. Carefully stir in 1/2 cup heavy cream (the mixture will bubble up) and cook, stirring, until smooth.
    3. Remove from heat and stir in 1 tablespoon of butter and 1/2 teaspoon vanilla extract. Let it cool to room temperature. For salted caramel, stir in a pinch of sea salt.
2. **Prepare the Ice Cream Base:**
    1. In a medium saucepan, combine the whole milk and heavy cream. Heat over medium heat until it begins to steam but does not boil.
    2. In a separate bowl, whisk together the egg yolks and granulated sugar until smooth and pale.
    3. Gradually whisk a small amount of the hot milk mixture into the egg yolks to temper them.
    4. Return the egg yolk mixture to the saucepan with the remaining milk mixture.
    5. Cook over medium heat, stirring constantly, until the mixture thickens slightly and coats the back of a spoon (about 5-7 minutes). Do not let it boil.
3. **Add Coffee Flavor:**
    1. Remove from heat and stir in the instant coffee or espresso powder until fully dissolved.
    2. Stir in the vanilla extract and a pinch of salt.
4. **Cool the Custard Base:**
    1. Pour the custard through a fine-mesh sieve into a clean bowl to remove any lumps.
    2. Allow the mixture to cool to room temperature.
    3. Cover and refrigerate for at least 2 hours, or until thoroughly chilled.
5. **Churn the Ice Cream:**
    1. Pour the chilled custard mixture into an ice cream maker and churn according to the manufacturer's instructions. This typically takes about 20-25 minutes, or until the ice cream reaches a soft-serve consistency.
6. **Add Caramel Swirl:**
    1. During the last few minutes of churning, drizzle in the caramel sauce, allowing it to swirl into the ice cream.

7. **Freeze:**
    1. Transfer the churned ice cream to an airtight container.
    2. Freeze for at least 2 hours, or until firm.
8. **Serve:**
    1. Scoop and enjoy your Caramel Macchiato Ice Cream! For an extra touch, you can drizzle additional caramel sauce on top or sprinkle with a bit of sea salt.

Enjoy the rich, creamy blend of caramel and coffee flavors in this indulgent ice cream, perfect for a sophisticated treat!

Lemon Blueberry Cheesecake Gelato

Ingredients:

For the Gelato Base:

- 1 1/2 cups whole milk
- 1 cup heavy cream
- 3/4 cup granulated sugar
- 1 cup cream cheese, softened
- 1 tablespoon lemon zest (about 1 lemon)

- 1 tablespoon freshly squeezed lemon juice
- 1 teaspoon vanilla extract
- A pinch of salt
- 4 large egg yolks

For the Blueberry Swirl:

- 1 1/2 cups fresh or frozen blueberries
- 1/4 cup granulated sugar
- 1 tablespoon freshly squeezed lemon juice
- 1 teaspoon lemon zest (optional)
- 1 tablespoon water

Instructions:

1. **Prepare the Blueberry Swirl:**
    1. In a medium saucepan, combine the blueberries, granulated sugar, lemon juice, and water.
    2. Cook over medium heat, stirring occasionally, until the blueberries break down and the mixture thickens (about 10-15 minutes).
    3. Remove from heat and let cool. For a smoother swirl, you can blend the mixture slightly or use a fine-mesh sieve to remove skins if desired.
2. **Prepare the Gelato Base:**
    1. In a medium saucepan, combine the whole milk and heavy cream. Heat over medium heat until it begins to steam but does not boil.
    2. In a separate bowl, whisk together the egg yolks and granulated sugar until smooth and pale.
    3. Gradually whisk a small amount of the hot milk mixture into the egg yolks to temper them.
    4. Return the egg yolk mixture to the saucepan with the remaining milk mixture.
    5. Cook over medium heat, stirring constantly, until the mixture thickens slightly and coats the back of a spoon (about 5-7 minutes). Do not let it boil.
3. **Add Cheesecake Flavor:**
    1. Remove from heat and stir in the softened cream cheese until smooth.
    2. Stir in the lemon zest, lemon juice, vanilla extract, and a pinch of salt.
4. **Cool the Custard Base:**
    1. Pour the custard through a fine-mesh sieve into a clean bowl to remove any lumps.
    2. Allow the mixture to cool to room temperature.
    3. Cover and refrigerate for at least 2 hours, or until thoroughly chilled.
5. **Churn the Gelato:**
    1. Pour the chilled custard mixture into an ice cream maker and churn according to the manufacturer's instructions. This typically takes about 20-25 minutes, or until the gelato reaches a soft-serve consistency.
6. **Add Blueberry Swirl:**

1. During the last few minutes of churning, gently swirl in the cooled blueberry mixture. You can swirl it lightly or fold it in to achieve your desired marbling effect.
7. **Freeze:**
    1. Transfer the churned gelato to an airtight container.
    2. Freeze for at least 2 hours, or until firm.
8. **Serve:**
    1. Scoop and enjoy your Lemon Blueberry Cheesecake Gelato! Garnish with additional lemon zest or fresh blueberries if desired.

Delight in the creamy, tangy, and fruity combination of lemon, blueberry, and cheesecake in this refreshing and indulgent gelato!

White Chocolate Ginger Frozen Yogurt

Ingredients:

- 2 cups plain Greek yogurt (full-fat or 2%)
- 1 cup white chocolate chips or chopped white chocolate
- 1/2 cup granulated sugar
- 1 tablespoon freshly grated ginger (or 1 teaspoon ground ginger)
- 1 teaspoon vanilla extract
- 1/2 cup milk (whole or 2%)
- A pinch of salt

Instructions:

1. **Melt the White Chocolate:**
    1. In a heatproof bowl, melt the white chocolate chips or chopped white chocolate over a pot of simmering water (double boiler method), stirring frequently until smooth. Alternatively, you can melt the chocolate in the microwave in 20-second intervals, stirring in between.
    2. Allow the melted white chocolate to cool slightly.
2. **Prepare the Yogurt Mixture:**
    1. In a large mixing bowl, combine the plain Greek yogurt, granulated sugar, freshly grated ginger (or ground ginger), and vanilla extract. Mix until the sugar is fully dissolved.
    2. Stir in the melted white chocolate until well combined.
    3. Gradually mix in the milk to achieve a smoother consistency. Add a pinch of salt and stir.
3. **Chill the Mixture:**
    1. Cover the bowl and refrigerate the mixture for at least 1-2 hours, or until thoroughly chilled.
4. **Churn the Frozen Yogurt:**
    1. Pour the chilled yogurt mixture into an ice cream maker and churn according to the manufacturer's instructions. This typically takes about 20-25 minutes, or until the yogurt reaches a soft-serve consistency.
5. **Freeze:**
    1. Transfer the churned frozen yogurt to an airtight container.
    2. Freeze for at least 2 hours, or until firm.
6. **Serve:**
    1. Scoop and enjoy your White Chocolate Ginger Frozen Yogurt! For an extra touch, you can garnish with a sprinkle of additional grated ginger or white chocolate shavings.

Enjoy the creamy, luxurious blend of white chocolate and spicy ginger in this refreshing frozen yogurt—perfect for a sophisticated and indulgent treat!

Classic Strawberry Ice Cream

Ingredients:

- 2 cups fresh strawberries, hulled and halved
- 3/4 cup granulated sugar
- 1 cup whole milk
- 1 cup heavy cream
- 1 teaspoon vanilla extract
- A pinch of salt
- 4 large egg yolks

Instructions:

1. **Prepare the Strawberry Mixture:**
    1. In a blender or food processor, blend the strawberries until smooth. If you prefer a chunkier texture, you can blend part of the strawberries and leave some in pieces.
    2. In a medium bowl, combine the strawberry puree with 1/2 cup of the granulated sugar. Stir until the sugar is dissolved. Set aside.
2. **Prepare the Ice Cream Base:**
    1. In a medium saucepan, combine the whole milk and heavy cream. Heat over medium heat until it begins to steam but does not boil.
    2. In a separate bowl, whisk together the egg yolks and the remaining 1/4 cup of granulated sugar until smooth and pale.
    3. Gradually whisk a small amount of the hot milk mixture into the egg yolks to temper them.
    4. Return the egg yolk mixture to the saucepan with the remaining milk mixture.
    5. Cook over medium heat, stirring constantly, until the mixture thickens slightly and coats the back of a spoon (about 5-7 minutes). Do not let it boil.
3. **Combine Strawberry and Custard:**
    1. Remove the custard mixture from heat and stir in the vanilla extract and a pinch of salt.
    2. Pour the custard through a fine-mesh sieve into the bowl with the strawberry mixture to remove any lumps.
    3. Stir until well combined.
4. **Cool the Mixture:**
    1. Allow the mixture to cool to room temperature.
    2. Cover and refrigerate for at least 2 hours, or until thoroughly chilled.
5. **Churn the Ice Cream:**
    1. Pour the chilled mixture into an ice cream maker and churn according to the manufacturer's instructions. This typically takes about 20-25 minutes, or until the ice cream reaches a soft-serve consistency.
6. **Freeze:**
    1. Transfer the churned ice cream to an airtight container.
    2. Freeze for at least 2 hours, or until firm.
7. **Serve:**
    1. Scoop and enjoy your Classic Strawberry Ice Cream! Garnish with fresh strawberry slices or a drizzle of strawberry sauce if desired.

Delight in the timeless combination of fresh strawberries and creamy ice cream, perfect for a classic and refreshing treat!

Mango Passionfruit Sorbet

Ingredients:

- 2 cups fresh or frozen mango chunks
- 1 cup passionfruit juice (fresh or store-bought)
- 1/2 cup granulated sugar (adjust to taste)
- 1/2 cup water
- 1 tablespoon freshly squeezed lime juice (optional, for added tang)
- A pinch of salt

Instructions:

1. **Prepare the Mango Puree:**
    1. In a blender or food processor, blend the mango chunks until smooth. If using frozen mango, ensure it's completely blended and creamy.
    2. If desired, you can strain the mango puree through a fine-mesh sieve to remove any fibrous bits, though this step is optional.
2. **Make the Sorbet Base:**
    1. In a medium saucepan, combine the granulated sugar and water. Heat over medium heat, stirring occasionally, until the sugar is completely dissolved. Allow the syrup to cool to room temperature.
    2. Stir the passionfruit juice into the cooled syrup. Add a pinch of salt.
3. **Combine Ingredients:**
    1. In a large mixing bowl, combine the mango puree with the passionfruit syrup mixture.
    2. Stir in the freshly squeezed lime juice if using, and mix until well combined.
4. **Chill the Mixture:**
    1. Cover the bowl and refrigerate the mixture for at least 1-2 hours, or until thoroughly chilled.
5. **Freeze the Sorbet:**
    1. Pour the chilled mixture into an ice cream maker and churn according to the manufacturer's instructions. This typically takes about 20-25 minutes, or until the sorbet reaches a soft-serve consistency.
6. **Freeze:**
    1. Transfer the churned sorbet to an airtight container.
    2. Freeze for at least 2 hours, or until firm.
7. **Serve:**
    1. Scoop and enjoy your Mango Passionfruit Sorbet! Garnish with fresh mint leaves or a few extra mango chunks if desired.

Enjoy the vibrant tropical flavors of mango and passionfruit in this refreshing and light sorbet, perfect for a sunny day or as a palate cleanser!

Tiramisu Gelato

Ingredients:

For the Gelato Base:

- 2 cups whole milk
- 1 cup heavy cream
- 3/4 cup granulated sugar
- 4 large egg yolks
- 1 teaspoon vanilla extract
- A pinch of salt

For the Mascarpone Mixture:

- 1 cup mascarpone cheese
- 1/2 cup granulated sugar
- 1 cup brewed espresso, cooled
- 1 tablespoon coffee liqueur (optional, such as Kahlua)
- 1 tablespoon unsweetened cocoa powder

For the Swirl:

- 1/2 cup chocolate shavings or chunks (optional)
- 1 tablespoon brewed espresso (optional, for a coffee swirl)

Instructions:

1. **Prepare the Gelato Base:**
    1. In a medium saucepan, combine the whole milk and heavy cream. Heat over medium heat until it begins to steam but does not boil.
    2. In a separate bowl, whisk together the egg yolks and granulated sugar until smooth and pale.
    3. Gradually whisk a small amount of the hot milk mixture into the egg yolks to temper them.
    4. Return the egg yolk mixture to the saucepan with the remaining milk mixture.
    5. Cook over medium heat, stirring constantly, until the mixture thickens slightly and coats the back of a spoon (about 5-7 minutes). Do not let it boil.
    6. Remove from heat and stir in the vanilla extract and a pinch of salt. Pour the custard through a fine-mesh sieve into a clean bowl to remove any lumps. Allow to cool to room temperature.
2. **Prepare the Mascarpone Mixture:**
    1. In a medium bowl, whisk together the mascarpone cheese and granulated sugar until smooth.
    2. Gradually whisk in the brewed espresso and coffee liqueur (if using) until fully combined. You may also add a tablespoon of brewed espresso to the gelato base if you want a stronger coffee flavor.
3. **Combine Mixtures:**
    1. Gently fold the mascarpone mixture into the cooled gelato base until well combined.
4. **Churn the Gelato:**
    1. Pour the mixture into an ice cream maker and churn according to the manufacturer's instructions. This typically takes about 20-25 minutes, or until the gelato reaches a soft-serve consistency.
5. **Add Swirls:**
    1. During the last few minutes of churning, add chocolate shavings or chunks to the gelato.

2. For a coffee swirl, drizzle in additional brewed espresso during the final churning phase, allowing it to ripple through the gelato.
6. **Freeze:**
   1. Transfer the churned gelato to an airtight container.
   2. Freeze for at least 2 hours, or until firm.
7. **Serve:**
   1. Scoop and enjoy your Tiramisu Gelato! Garnish with a dusting of unsweetened cocoa powder or additional chocolate shavings if desired.

Indulge in the creamy, coffee-infused flavors of classic tiramisu transformed into a smooth and decadent gelato, perfect for a refined dessert treat!

Fig and Honey Ice Cream

Ingredients:

- 1 1/2 cups fresh figs, chopped (or 1 cup dried figs, chopped and soaked in hot water)
- 1 cup whole milk
- 1 cup heavy cream
- 3/4 cup granulated sugar
- 1/4 cup honey
- 1 teaspoon vanilla extract
- A pinch of salt
- 4 large egg yolks

Instructions:

1. **Prepare the Fig Mixture:**
    1. If using fresh figs, wash and chop them. If using dried figs, soak them in hot water for about 30 minutes to soften, then chop.
    2. In a medium saucepan, cook the chopped figs over medium heat with a splash of water, stirring occasionally, until they are soft and the mixture is slightly thickened (about 10 minutes). Allow to cool slightly.
2. **Prepare the Ice Cream Base:**
    1. In a medium saucepan, combine the whole milk and heavy cream. Heat over medium heat until it begins to steam but does not boil.
    2. In a separate bowl, whisk together the egg yolks and granulated sugar until smooth and pale.
    3. Gradually whisk a small amount of the hot milk mixture into the egg yolks to temper them.
    4. Return the egg yolk mixture to the saucepan with the remaining milk mixture.
    5. Cook over medium heat, stirring constantly, until the mixture thickens slightly and coats the back of a spoon (about 5-7 minutes). Do not let it boil.
    6. Remove from heat and stir in the honey, vanilla extract, and a pinch of salt. Allow to cool slightly.
3. **Combine Mixtures:**
    1. Stir the fig mixture into the cooled custard base until well combined.
4. **Chill the Mixture:**
    1. Pour the mixture through a fine-mesh sieve into a clean bowl to remove any larger pieces of fig.
    2. Cover and refrigerate the mixture for at least 2 hours, or until thoroughly chilled.
5. **Churn the Ice Cream:**
    1. Pour the chilled mixture into an ice cream maker and churn according to the manufacturer's instructions. This typically takes about 20-25 minutes, or until the ice cream reaches a soft-serve consistency.
6. **Freeze:**
    1. Transfer the churned ice cream to an airtight container.
    2. Freeze for at least 2 hours, or until firm.
7. **Serve:**
    1. Scoop and enjoy your Fig and Honey Ice Cream! For an extra touch, you can drizzle a bit of honey on top or garnish with a few fresh fig slices if available.

Enjoy the rich, sweet flavors of figs and honey in this creamy ice cream, perfect for a sophisticated and delightful dessert!

Matcha Red Bean Sorbet

Ingredients:

For the Sorbet Base:

- 2 cups water
- 1 cup granulated sugar
- 1 tablespoon matcha green tea powder
- 1/2 teaspoon vanilla extract
- A pinch of salt

For the Red Bean Mixture:

- 1 cup red bean paste (sweetened adzuki bean paste, store-bought or homemade)
- 1/2 cup water
- 1 tablespoon granulated sugar (if needed)

Instructions:

1. **Prepare the Red Bean Mixture:**
    1. In a small saucepan, combine the red bean paste and 1/2 cup water. Heat over medium heat, stirring frequently, until the mixture is smooth and well combined. If the paste is too thick, add a little more water to reach a smooth consistency.
    2. Taste and adjust sweetness if needed by stirring in additional granulated sugar. Allow the mixture to cool to room temperature.
2. **Prepare the Sorbet Base:**
    1. In a medium saucepan, combine 2 cups water and 1 cup granulated sugar. Heat over medium heat, stirring occasionally, until the sugar is completely dissolved. Allow the syrup to cool to room temperature.
    2. Once cooled, whisk in the matcha powder, vanilla extract, and a pinch of salt until fully dissolved and smooth.
3. **Combine Mixtures:**
    1. Stir the red bean mixture into the cooled matcha syrup until well combined.
4. **Chill the Mixture:**
    1. Cover the mixture and refrigerate for at least 1-2 hours, or until thoroughly chilled.
5. **Freeze the Sorbet:**
    1. Pour the chilled mixture into an ice cream maker and churn according to the manufacturer's instructions. This typically takes about 20-25 minutes, or until the sorbet reaches a soft-serve consistency.
6. **Freeze:**
    1. Transfer the churned sorbet to an airtight container.
    2. Freeze for at least 2 hours, or until firm.
7. **Serve:**
    1. Scoop and enjoy your Matcha Red Bean Sorbet! For added texture, you can gently fold in small spoonfuls of red bean paste into the sorbet before freezing.

Indulge in the unique fusion of earthy matcha and sweet red beans with this refreshing and creamy sorbet, perfect for a sophisticated treat!

S'mores Frozen Custard

Ingredients:

For the Custard Base:

- 2 cups whole milk
- 1 cup heavy cream
- 3/4 cup granulated sugar
- 4 large egg yolks
- 1 teaspoon vanilla extract
- A pinch of salt

For the S'mores Mix-Ins:

- 1 cup graham cracker crumbs

- 1 cup mini marshmallows (or 1/2 cup regular marshmallows, chopped)
- 1/2 cup chocolate chips or chopped chocolate
- 1/4 cup heavy cream (for the chocolate swirl, optional)

Instructions:

1. **Prepare the Custard Base:**
    1. In a medium saucepan, combine the whole milk and heavy cream. Heat over medium heat until it begins to steam but does not boil.
    2. In a separate bowl, whisk together the egg yolks and granulated sugar until smooth and pale.
    3. Gradually whisk a small amount of the hot milk mixture into the egg yolks to temper them.
    4. Return the egg yolk mixture to the saucepan with the remaining milk mixture.
    5. Cook over medium heat, stirring constantly, until the mixture thickens slightly and coats the back of a spoon (about 5-7 minutes). Do not let it boil.
    6. Remove from heat and stir in the vanilla extract and a pinch of salt. Allow to cool slightly.
2. **Chill the Custard Base:**
    1. Pour the custard through a fine-mesh sieve into a clean bowl to remove any lumps.
    2. Cover and refrigerate for at least 2 hours, or until thoroughly chilled.
3. **Prepare the Chocolate Swirl (Optional):**
    1. In a small saucepan, heat 1/4 cup heavy cream until it begins to steam.
    2. Remove from heat and stir in chocolate chips or chopped chocolate until fully melted and smooth.
    3. Allow the chocolate mixture to cool to room temperature.
4. **Churn the Custard:**
    1. Pour the chilled custard base into an ice cream maker and churn according to the manufacturer's instructions. This typically takes about 20-25 minutes, or until the custard reaches a soft-serve consistency.
5. **Add S'mores Mix-Ins:**
    1. During the last few minutes of churning, gently fold in the graham cracker crumbs and mini marshmallows.
    2. If using, drizzle the cooled chocolate swirl over the custard and fold gently to create a marbled effect.
6. **Freeze:**
    1. Transfer the churned custard to an airtight container.
    2. Freeze for at least 2 hours, or until firm.
7. **Serve:**
    1. Scoop and enjoy your S'mores Frozen Custard! For an extra touch, you can garnish with additional graham cracker crumbs, mini marshmallows, or a drizzle of chocolate syrup.

Enjoy the creamy, nostalgic flavors of s'mores in this indulgent frozen custard—perfect for a summer treat or a cozy dessert!

Pineapple Mint Gelato

Ingredients:

- 2 cups fresh pineapple chunks (or canned pineapple, drained)
- 1 cup whole milk
- 1 cup heavy cream
- 3/4 cup granulated sugar
- 1/4 cup honey (or agave syrup)
- 1/4 cup fresh mint leaves (loosely packed)
- 1 teaspoon vanilla extract
- A pinch of salt

Instructions:

1. **Prepare the Pineapple Puree:**

1. In a blender or food processor, blend the pineapple chunks until smooth. If you prefer a chunkier texture, blend part of the pineapple and leave some in pieces.
   2. Strain the pineapple puree through a fine-mesh sieve into a bowl to remove any fibrous bits, if desired.
2. **Infuse the Mint:**
   1. In a small saucepan, heat the whole milk and heavy cream over medium heat until it begins to steam but does not boil.
   2. Add the fresh mint leaves to the milk and cream mixture. Remove from heat and let it steep for about 10-15 minutes, allowing the mint to infuse its flavor.
   3. Strain out the mint leaves and return the infused milk and cream mixture to the saucepan.
3. **Make the Gelato Base:**
   1. Stir in the granulated sugar and honey (or agave syrup) into the warm milk and cream mixture. Heat gently, stirring occasionally, until the sugar is completely dissolved. Allow the mixture to cool slightly.
   2. Stir in the vanilla extract and a pinch of salt.
4. **Combine Ingredients:**
   1. In a large mixing bowl, combine the pineapple puree with the cooled milk and cream mixture. Stir until well combined.
5. **Chill the Mixture:**
   1. Cover the mixture and refrigerate for at least 2 hours, or until thoroughly chilled.
6. **Churn the Gelato:**
   1. Pour the chilled mixture into an ice cream maker and churn according to the manufacturer's instructions. This typically takes about 20-25 minutes, or until the gelato reaches a soft-serve consistency.
7. **Freeze:**
   1. Transfer the churned gelato to an airtight container.
   2. Freeze for at least 2 hours, or until firm.
8. **Serve:**
   1. Scoop and enjoy your Pineapple Mint Gelato! For added garnish, you can top with fresh mint leaves or a sprinkle of toasted coconut.

Delight in the refreshing blend of tropical pineapple and cool mint in this smooth, creamy gelato—perfect for a refreshing summer treat!

Chai Tea Ice Cream

Ingredients:

- 2 cups whole milk
- 1 cup heavy cream
- 3/4 cup granulated sugar
- 4 large egg yolks
- 2 tablespoons loose chai tea leaves or 2 chai tea bags
- 1 teaspoon vanilla extract
- A pinch of salt

Instructions:

1. **Infuse the Milk and Cream:**

1. In a medium saucepan, combine the whole milk and heavy cream. Heat over medium heat until it begins to steam but does not boil.
2. Add the chai tea leaves or tea bags to the milk and cream mixture. Remove from heat and let it steep for 10-15 minutes to infuse the flavors.
3. If using loose tea leaves, strain them out by pouring the mixture through a fine-mesh sieve into a bowl. If using tea bags, remove them and discard.

2. **Prepare the Custard Base:**
    1. In a separate bowl, whisk together the egg yolks and granulated sugar until smooth and pale.
    2. Gradually whisk a small amount of the hot milk mixture into the egg yolks to temper them.
    3. Return the egg yolk mixture to the saucepan with the remaining milk mixture.
    4. Cook over medium heat, stirring constantly, until the mixture thickens slightly and coats the back of a spoon (about 5-7 minutes). Do not let it boil.
    5. Remove from heat and stir in the vanilla extract and a pinch of salt. Allow the custard base to cool slightly.
3. **Chill the Custard Base:**
    1. Pour the custard through a fine-mesh sieve into a clean bowl to remove any lumps.
    2. Cover and refrigerate for at least 2 hours, or until thoroughly chilled.
4. **Churn the Ice Cream:**
    1. Pour the chilled custard base into an ice cream maker and churn according to the manufacturer's instructions. This typically takes about 20-25 minutes, or until the ice cream reaches a soft-serve consistency.
5. **Freeze:**
    1. Transfer the churned ice cream to an airtight container.
    2. Freeze for at least 2 hours, or until firm.
6. **Serve:**
    1. Scoop and enjoy your Chai Tea Ice Cream! For added spice, you can garnish with a sprinkle of ground cinnamon or cardamom.

Indulge in the warm, aromatic flavors of chai tea in this creamy and comforting ice cream, perfect for a cozy dessert or an exotic treat!

Pear Vanilla Sorbet

Ingredients:

- 4 cups fresh pear juice (from about 6-8 ripe pears) or 4 cups canned pear juice
- 1 cup granulated sugar
- 1 tablespoon freshly squeezed lemon juice
- 1 tablespoon vanilla extract
- A pinch of salt

Instructions:

1. **Prepare the Pear Juice:**

1. If using fresh pears, peel, core, and chop them. Blend the chopped pears in a blender or food processor until smooth. Strain the puree through a fine-mesh sieve to obtain fresh pear juice. You should have about 4 cups of juice.
2. If using canned pear juice, ensure it is well-drained and free of any added sugars.

2. **Make the Sorbet Base:**
   1. In a medium saucepan, combine the pear juice and granulated sugar. Heat over medium heat, stirring occasionally, until the sugar is completely dissolved. This usually takes about 5 minutes.
   2. Remove from heat and stir in the freshly squeezed lemon juice, vanilla extract, and a pinch of salt.
3. **Chill the Mixture:**
   1. Allow the mixture to cool to room temperature.
   2. Cover and refrigerate for at least 2 hours, or until thoroughly chilled.
4. **Freeze the Sorbet:**
   1. Pour the chilled mixture into an ice cream maker and churn according to the manufacturer's instructions. This typically takes about 20-25 minutes, or until the sorbet reaches a soft-serve consistency.
5. **Freeze:**
   1. Transfer the churned sorbet to an airtight container.
   2. Freeze for at least 2 hours, or until firm.
6. **Serve:**
   1. Scoop and enjoy your Pear Vanilla Sorbet! Garnish with fresh pear slices or a sprig of mint for a lovely presentation.

Enjoy the light, refreshing flavors of ripe pears combined with a hint of vanilla in this elegant sorbet—perfect for a fruity and refreshing treat!

Dark Chocolate Chili Ice Cream

Ingredients:

- 1 1/2 cups whole milk
- 1 1/2 cups heavy cream
- 3/4 cup granulated sugar
- 1/2 cup unsweetened cocoa powder
- 4 ounces dark chocolate (70% or higher), chopped
- 4 large egg yolks
- 1/2 teaspoon ground chili powder (adjust to taste)
- 1/4 teaspoon ground cinnamon (optional, for added warmth)

- 1 teaspoon vanilla extract
- A pinch of salt

Instructions:

1. **Prepare the Chocolate Mixture:**
    1. In a medium saucepan, combine the whole milk and heavy cream. Heat over medium heat until it begins to steam but does not boil.
    2. Remove from heat and whisk in the unsweetened cocoa powder until fully dissolved.
    3. Stir in the chopped dark chocolate until completely melted and smooth. Allow the mixture to cool slightly.
2. **Prepare the Custard Base:**
    1. In a separate bowl, whisk together the egg yolks and granulated sugar until smooth and pale.
    2. Gradually whisk a small amount of the hot chocolate mixture into the egg yolks to temper them.
    3. Return the egg yolk mixture to the saucepan with the remaining chocolate mixture.
    4. Cook over medium heat, stirring constantly, until the mixture thickens slightly and coats the back of a spoon (about 5-7 minutes). Do not let it boil.
    5. Remove from heat and stir in the ground chili powder, ground cinnamon (if using), vanilla extract, and a pinch of salt. Allow the custard base to cool slightly.
3. **Chill the Custard Base:**
    1. Pour the custard through a fine-mesh sieve into a clean bowl to remove any lumps.
    2. Cover and refrigerate for at least 2 hours, or until thoroughly chilled.
4. **Churn the Ice Cream:**
    1. Pour the chilled custard base into an ice cream maker and churn according to the manufacturer's instructions. This typically takes about 20-25 minutes, or until the ice cream reaches a soft-serve consistency.
5. **Freeze:**
    1. Transfer the churned ice cream to an airtight container.
    2. Freeze for at least 2 hours, or until firm.
6. **Serve:**
    1. Scoop and enjoy your Dark Chocolate Chili Ice Cream! For an extra kick, you can sprinkle a little more chili powder on top or garnish with dark chocolate shavings.

Experience the bold combination of rich dark chocolate and a spicy kick in this decadent ice cream—perfect for those who love a little heat with their sweets!

Coconut Lychee Gelato

Ingredients:

- 1 1/2 cups canned coconut milk (full-fat)
- 1 cup heavy cream
- 1 cup granulated sugar
- 1 cup fresh or canned lychee fruit (drained, if canned)
- 1 tablespoon freshly squeezed lime juice
- 1 teaspoon vanilla extract
- A pinch of salt

Instructions:

1. **Prepare the Lychee Puree:**
    1. If using fresh lychee, peel and remove the seeds from the fruit. Blend the lychee fruit in a blender or food processor until smooth. If using canned lychee, drain and blend until smooth.
    2. Strain the lychee puree through a fine-mesh sieve to ensure a smooth texture.
2. **Make the Gelato Base:**
    1. In a medium saucepan, combine the coconut milk, heavy cream, and granulated sugar. Heat over medium heat, stirring occasionally, until the sugar is completely dissolved and the mixture is warm but not boiling.
    2. Remove from heat and stir in the lychee puree, lime juice, vanilla extract, and a pinch of salt. Mix until fully combined.
3. **Chill the Mixture:**
    1. Allow the mixture to cool to room temperature.
    2. Cover and refrigerate for at least 2 hours, or until thoroughly chilled.
4. **Churn the Gelato:**
    1. Pour the chilled mixture into an ice cream maker and churn according to the manufacturer's instructions. This typically takes about 20-25 minutes, or until the gelato reaches a soft-serve consistency.
5. **Freeze:**
    1. Transfer the churned gelato to an airtight container.
    2. Freeze for at least 2 hours, or until firm.
6. **Serve:**
    1. Scoop and enjoy your Coconut Lychee Gelato! Garnish with toasted coconut flakes or a few fresh lychee slices if desired.

Savor the exotic blend of creamy coconut and sweet lychee in this refreshing and tropical gelato—ideal for a light and indulgent treat!

Blackberry Lemonade Granita

Ingredients:

- 2 cups fresh blackberries (or frozen, thawed)
- 1 cup freshly squeezed lemon juice (about 4-6 lemons)
- 1 cup granulated sugar
- 1 cup water
- 1/2 teaspoon lemon zest (optional, for added lemon flavor)
- A pinch of salt

Instructions:

1. **Prepare the Blackberry Puree:**
    1. In a blender or food processor, blend the blackberries until smooth.
    2. Strain the puree through a fine-mesh sieve into a bowl to remove the seeds.
2. **Make the Lemonade Base:**
    1. In a medium saucepan, combine the water and granulated sugar. Heat over medium heat, stirring occasionally, until the sugar is completely dissolved. Allow the mixture to cool to room temperature.
    2. Stir in the freshly squeezed lemon juice and lemon zest (if using). Mix until well combined.
3. **Combine and Freeze:**
    1. Stir the blackberry puree into the lemon mixture until well combined.
    2. Pour the mixture into a shallow dish (such as a baking pan) that will fit in your freezer.
    3. Freeze for about 1 hour, then use a fork to scrape and stir the mixture, breaking up any ice crystals that are forming.
    4. Continue to freeze, scraping with a fork every 30 minutes, until the granita is fully frozen and has a fluffy, crystalline texture. This usually takes about 3-4 hours.
4. **Serve:**
    1. Once the granita is ready, scrape it with a fork to fluff the crystals before serving.
    2. Scoop into glasses or bowls and enjoy! Garnish with fresh blackberries or a mint sprig if desired.

Enjoy the refreshing combination of tart lemonade and sweet blackberries in this easy-to-make granita, perfect for a cooling summer treat or a light dessert!

Banana Cream Pie Gelato

Ingredients:

For the Gelato Base:

- 1 1/2 cups whole milk
- 1 1/2 cups heavy cream
- 3/4 cup granulated sugar
- 1/2 cup ripe banana puree (about 2 medium bananas)
- 1/2 teaspoon vanilla extract
- 1/4 teaspoon ground cinnamon (optional, for added flavor)
- A pinch of salt

For the Pie Crust Swirl:

- 1/2 cup graham cracker crumbs
- 2 tablespoons granulated sugar
- 2 tablespoons unsalted butter, melted

For the Banana Ripple (Optional):

- 1/2 cup banana puree (about 1 banana)
- 1/4 cup granulated sugar
- 1 teaspoon lemon juice

Instructions:

1. **Prepare the Pie Crust Swirl:**
    1. In a small bowl, mix together the graham cracker crumbs, granulated sugar, and melted butter until the crumbs are evenly coated.
    2. Set aside.
2. **Make the Gelato Base:**
    1. In a medium saucepan, combine the whole milk, heavy cream, and granulated sugar. Heat over medium heat, stirring occasionally, until the sugar is completely dissolved and the mixture is warm but not boiling.
    2. Remove from heat and stir in the ripe banana puree, vanilla extract, ground cinnamon (if using), and a pinch of salt. Mix until fully combined.
3. **Chill the Mixture:**
    1. Allow the mixture to cool to room temperature.
    2. Cover and refrigerate for at least 2 hours, or until thoroughly chilled.
4. **Prepare the Banana Ripple (Optional):**
    1. In a small bowl, combine the banana puree, granulated sugar, and lemon juice. Stir until the sugar is dissolved. Set aside.
5. **Churn the Gelato:**
    1. Pour the chilled gelato base into an ice cream maker and churn according to the manufacturer's instructions. This typically takes about 20-25 minutes, or until the gelato reaches a soft-serve consistency.
6. **Add Mix-Ins and Freeze:**
    1. If using the banana ripple, gently swirl it into the churned gelato with a spoon or spatula.
    2. Fold in the graham cracker crumb mixture to distribute it throughout the gelato.
    3. Transfer the gelato to an airtight container.
    4. Freeze for at least 2 hours, or until firm.
7. **Serve:**
    1. Scoop and enjoy your Banana Cream Pie Gelato! For a garnish, you can add additional graham cracker crumbs or banana slices if desired.

Enjoy the creamy, nostalgic flavors of banana cream pie in this rich and smooth gelato—perfect for a delightful dessert or a special treat!

Classic Pistachio Gelato

Ingredients:

- 1 cup shelled pistachios (unsalted)
- 1 1/2 cups whole milk
- 1 1/2 cups heavy cream
- 3/4 cup granulated sugar
- 4 large egg yolks
- 1 teaspoon vanilla extract
- A pinch of salt

Instructions:

1. **Prepare the Pistachio Paste:**
    1. In a food processor or blender, finely grind the pistachios until they form a coarse paste. You can add a bit of sugar or milk if needed to help with blending.
2. **Make the Gelato Base:**
    1. In a medium saucepan, combine the whole milk and heavy cream. Heat over medium heat until the mixture begins to steam but does not boil.
    2. In a separate bowl, whisk together the egg yolks and granulated sugar until smooth and pale.
    3. Gradually whisk a small amount of the hot milk mixture into the egg yolks to temper them.
    4. Return the egg yolk mixture to the saucepan with the remaining milk mixture.
    5. Cook over medium heat, stirring constantly, until the mixture thickens slightly and coats the back of a spoon (about 5-7 minutes). Do not let it boil.
    6. Remove from heat and stir in the pistachio paste, vanilla extract, and a pinch of salt. Mix until fully combined and smooth.
3. **Chill the Mixture:**
    1. Pour the custard through a fine-mesh sieve into a clean bowl to remove any lumps.
    2. Cover and refrigerate for at least 2 hours, or until thoroughly chilled.
4. **Churn the Gelato:**
    1. Pour the chilled mixture into an ice cream maker and churn according to the manufacturer's instructions. This typically takes about 20-25 minutes, or until the gelato reaches a soft-serve consistency.
5. **Freeze:**
    1. Transfer the churned gelato to an airtight container.
    2. Freeze for at least 2 hours, or until firm.
6. **Serve:**
    1. Scoop and enjoy your Classic Pistachio Gelato! For an extra touch, garnish with a few whole pistachios or a sprinkle of finely chopped pistachios.

Enjoy the rich, nutty flavor of pistachios in this creamy, traditional gelato—perfect for a classic and elegant dessert!

Maple Pecan Ice Cream

Ingredients:

- 1 cup pecans, chopped
- 1 1/2 cups whole milk
- 1 1/2 cups heavy cream
- 3/4 cup pure maple syrup
- 1/2 cup granulated sugar
- 4 large egg yolks
- 1 teaspoon vanilla extract
- A pinch of salt

Instructions:

1. **Toast the Pecans:**

1. Preheat your oven to 350°F (175°C).
2. Spread the chopped pecans on a baking sheet in a single layer.
3. Toast in the oven for 5-7 minutes, or until fragrant and lightly browned, stirring halfway through to ensure even toasting.
4. Allow the pecans to cool to room temperature.

2. **Make the Ice Cream Base:**
    1. In a medium saucepan, combine the whole milk and heavy cream. Heat over medium heat until the mixture begins to steam but does not boil.
    2. In a separate bowl, whisk together the egg yolks and granulated sugar until smooth and pale.
    3. Gradually whisk a small amount of the hot milk mixture into the egg yolks to temper them.
    4. Return the egg yolk mixture to the saucepan with the remaining milk mixture.
    5. Cook over medium heat, stirring constantly, until the mixture thickens slightly and coats the back of a spoon (about 5-7 minutes). Do not let it boil.
    6. Remove from heat and stir in the pure maple syrup, vanilla extract, and a pinch of salt. Mix until well combined.

3. **Chill the Mixture:**
    1. Pour the custard through a fine-mesh sieve into a clean bowl to remove any lumps.
    2. Cover and refrigerate for at least 2 hours, or until thoroughly chilled.

4. **Churn the Ice Cream:**
    1. Pour the chilled mixture into an ice cream maker and churn according to the manufacturer's instructions. This typically takes about 20-25 minutes, or until the ice cream reaches a soft-serve consistency.

5. **Add the Pecans:**
    1. During the last 5 minutes of churning, add the toasted pecans to the ice cream maker.

6. **Freeze:**
    1. Transfer the churned ice cream to an airtight container.
    2. Freeze for at least 2 hours, or until firm.

7. **Serve:**
    1. Scoop and enjoy your Maple Pecan Ice Cream! For an extra touch, you can drizzle with a bit more maple syrup or sprinkle additional chopped pecans on top.

Enjoy the rich, sweet flavor of maple syrup combined with the nutty crunch of toasted pecans in this creamy, indulgent ice cream!

Matcha Lemon Sorbet

Ingredients:

- 1 cup freshly squeezed lemon juice (about 4-6 lemons)
- 1 cup granulated sugar
- 2 tablespoons matcha green tea powder
- 1 1/2 cups water
- 1 teaspoon lemon zest (optional, for added lemon flavor)
- A pinch of salt

Instructions:

1. **Prepare the Lemon Base:**

1. In a medium saucepan, combine the water and granulated sugar. Heat over medium heat, stirring occasionally, until the sugar is completely dissolved. Allow the mixture to cool to room temperature.
2. Stir in the freshly squeezed lemon juice and lemon zest (if using).

2. **Incorporate the Matcha:**
    1. In a small bowl, whisk the matcha green tea powder with a few tablespoons of the lemon mixture to create a smooth paste. This will help to dissolve the matcha evenly and avoid clumps.
    2. Stir the matcha paste into the remaining lemon mixture until fully combined.

3. **Chill the Mixture:**
    1. Cover the mixture and refrigerate for at least 2 hours, or until thoroughly chilled.

4. **Freeze the Sorbet:**
    1. Pour the chilled mixture into a shallow dish (such as a baking pan) that will fit in your freezer.
    2. Freeze for about 1 hour, then use a fork to scrape and stir the mixture, breaking up any ice crystals that are forming.
    3. Continue to freeze, scraping with a fork every 30 minutes, until the sorbet is fully frozen and has a fluffy, crystalline texture. This usually takes about 3-4 hours.

5. **Serve:**
    1. Once the sorbet is ready, scrape it with a fork to fluff the crystals before serving.
    2. Scoop into glasses or bowls and enjoy! Garnish with a mint sprig or additional lemon zest if desired.

Enjoy the refreshing and vibrant flavors of matcha and lemon in this zesty and cooling sorbet—perfect for a light and invigorating treat!

www.ingramcontent.com/pod-product-compliance
Lightning Source LLC
LaVergne TN
LVHW081612060526
838201LV00054B/2218

9798330328253